CW00641438

BY ACCIDENT OR DESIGN

BY ACCIDENT OR DESIGN

Challenges and coincidences in my life

Rosemary Sassoon

intellect Bristol, UK / Chicago, USA

First published in the UK in 2018 by
Intellect, The Mill, Parnall Road, Fishponds, Bristol, BS16 3JG, UK

First published in the USA in 2018 by
Intellect, The University of Chicago Press, 1427 E. 60th Street,
Chicago, IL 60637, USA

Copyright © 2018 Intellect Ltd.

All rights reserved. No part of this publication may be reproduced,
stored in a retrieval system, or transmitted, in any form or by
any means, electronic, mechanical, photocopying, recording, or
otherwise, without written permission.

A catalogue record for this book is available from the
British Library.

Cover designer: Mike Blacker
Design & typesetting: Mike Blacker
Production manager: Tim Mitchell

Print ISBN: 978-1-78320-866-1
ePDF ISBN: 978-1-78320-867-8
ePUB ISBN: 978-1-78320-890-6

Printed and bound by CPI Group Ltd, Croydon, UK.

Contents

Part 1

Early life and design work

Introduction

It is always said that our characters are formed partly by nature and partly by nurture. Today our genes are probably mostly held responsible, but even that seems simplistic. What about coincidences and other happenings quite outside our control? My education could be termed a casualty of the Second World War, and it seems to me that my whole adult life has been influenced by a series of coincidences. A discarded newspaper led me to a new design job when I was desperate, an offer to write a book came out of the blue, then a somewhat inappropriate and an unwanted request to deal with handwriting problems, at first educational and then medical, led to a whole new career. I did not seek any of these opportunities. They just fell into my lap, and in doing so pushed my area of interest out wider and wider, until I have got to the stage now that when people ask me what is my profession I do not know how to answer.

In this book I will try to record how this all occurred. When I started out, in the late 1940s, few women were expected to have a meaningful career. A few good teachers along the way, and later good mentors certainly helped, but I consider myself extremely lucky to have had such a satisfying and productive career. It was all rather like my husband who said that he had never done a days work in his life that he would not have done for nothing – except that I quite often actually had to work for nothing!

Early life

As for nurture, my family was fairly conventional, probably typical of the time between the wars. I was the third girl of parents who really only wanted sons, in other words, the last straw. Born in 1931, I lived in the nursery, looked after by my much-loved nanny and saw little of my parents in my early days. Nanny stayed as a valued member of the family until the end of her life, being there to see all our children born as well. My background was fairly international. My maternal grandfather was Russian. He was a diplomat who dealt with the problems following the Russian-Japanese War. Then, luckily, he was in the embassy in Washington during the years of the revolution, before returning to live in London.

My father's grandfather was the ancestor I really wish I had known. He was a musician and artist with many interests, but sadly he died very young. Why his son, my gentle grandfather, joined the stock exchange I cannot understand. The story is that he only prospered because friends loved him and sent him business. After being in the army in the First World War, my father, Frank Waley, joined his father in the family firm. A practical man, I am sure he would have been happier as an architect or almost anything else. He spent much of his spare time, rather like a Victorian plant hunter, exploring the mountain ranges of Europe. He looked for unknown species of plants and brought then back to England to naturalize. In spring his garden was covered with rare narcissi, cyclamen and other bulbs that sometimes bore his name. His beloved garden contributed to his end at the age of 94. At the end of the 1980s the south of England was struck by a hurricane. It blew down the pine trees that grew on his hillside garden. Still strong, he rushed out to try and to pull the trunks off his precious shrubs. He suffered a mild heart attack but refused treatment saying that if his garden was ruined he did not want to go on.

My mother, who had had an unusual childhood travelling the world, spoke several languages, and deserved to have had a much more interesting life and career. However, constrained by the times, her main interest was playing bridge. In later life, almost every day she drove twenty-six miles to London to play at the well-known club, Crockfords, more or less as a professional. Travel, her dogs, her flowers, and later her vegetable garden kept her relatively content. Compared with her life, her two close cousins who came out of Russia in very straightened circumstances, both had satisfying careers. There were relations on both sides of the family all over Europe for us to visit after the war. My favourites, apart from my French godmother, lived in Denmark.

BY ORDER OF THE EXECUTORS OF THE LATE SIR JOHN KIRK.   SALE NO. 336.

SEVENOAKS.

Within 10 Minutes walk of the Station, with its 30 Minutes Express Service to the City and West End.

Particulars and Conditions of Sale of the

Substantially-Built Modern

Freehold Residence

KNOWN AS

"Wavertree"

MOUNT HARRY ROAD

Occupying an Elevated Position on Sandy Soil and Enjoying magnificent Views over a wide area of well-wooded and undulating country.

containing:

3 RECEPTION ROOMS   SERVANTS' HALL
GOOD OFFICES   10 BEDROOMS and BATHROOM

PICTURESQUE PLEASURE GROUNDS.

With Rhododendron Walks, fine Specimen and Timber Trees, good Kitchen Garden, &c., in all extending to about

2½ ACRES

Company's Gas & Water. Main Drainage. Electric Light Available.
VACANT POSSESSION ON COMPLETION.

WHICH

Messrs F. D. IBBETT & Co.

IN CONJUNCTION WITH

Messrs. RALPH PAY & TAYLOR

Are instructed to Sell by Auction,

At the London Auction Mart, 155, Queen Victoria Street, E.C. 4.

On Wednesday, 11th April, 1923

At 2.30 p.m., (unless previously Sold by Private Treaty)

Particulars and Conditions of Sale may be obtained of the Solicitors :

Messrs. Knocker, Knocker & Foskett, Sevenoaks, and of the Auctioneers,
Messrs. Ralph Pay & Taylor, 3, Mount Street, Grosvenor Square, London, W. 1 and
Messrs. F. D. Ibbett & Co., F.A.I., Sevenoaks & Oxted.   Telephone: Sevenoaks 147.

The Caxton Press, High Street, Sevenoaks.

The advertisement for the sale of the large red brick house that my parents purchased in 1923 where I spent my early years.

Before the war we lived in a large, rather ugly redbrick Victorian house, perched on a hill conveniently above Sevenoaks station. From the 1923 advertisement you can see it had eight bedrooms but only one bathroom. By the time we lived in it, it had several more bathrooms. I remember the main bedroom and a spare room for visitors plus three nursery rooms. I suspect the three attic rooms were originally intended for servants. The entire road had been built up at the time of the coming of the railway, expressly for the purpose of those who wished to commute – not that it would have been called that in those days. My father went to the city each day and returned early probably to tend his beloved plants. His view of the garden differed somewhat from ours. Sir John Kirk, an African explorer, had lived in the house before my parents bought it. He had planted a large grove of bamboos to house a collection of skeletons of big game. It remained as a somewhat unusual playground for us.

At the bottom of the hill, just opposite the station was the site of Sevenoaks market that took place every Monday. As we got older this was another exciting place to explore. Early in the war the cattle and sheep pens were used to house the hundreds of children ready to be evacuated to safer parts of the country.

In 1938, when I was seven, the house was sold and a modern one erected on half the garden. My mother was delighted, she got what she had always wanted, a white house. It was not to keep its pristine colour for long – a white house on the top of a hill above a railway was too good a guide for bombers on the way to London. It had to be camouflaged, and remained a dirty khaki colour for quite a few years. The old house was occupied by a succession of evacuees and was eventually demolished and replaced by a hideous post war block of flats. My father was in the army again in the Second World War, not abroad, but as a staff officer in the south of England. Those years were strangely some of my mother's happiest – doing real jobs like fire watching. She also grew and harvested potatoes on a large plot of land, as her contribution to the war effort, as well as growing all the family food in the garden.

As for me, at the age of about four I went to a kindergarten, nursery school or whatever they were called in those days, run by a remarkable lady called Miss Evans who had previously been a governess to Nigel Nicolson at Sissinghurst Castle. In the next couple of years I must have learned to read and write, as I still have some little books that I won as prizes there. The only distinct memories of those happy years are of the subtly coloured sketchbooks that we used when learning to observe and draw flowers and simple objects. Real school was a disappointment, and I remember surprisingly little of the next few years. I just have a vague memory of a large bullying classroom teacher and some uncomfortable mats that were put on the floor for us to

My mother took these pictures in 1939 when children were waiting to be evacuated, herded in the sheep and cattle pens of Sevenoaks market.

rest on after lunch. I cannot remember much of how or what we were taught. I find, in retrospect that it is only the happy memories of those early years that remain. My last memory was of the trenches being dug in the playground just before the war disrupted my education.

After a brief stay in Dorset at the height of the blitz, we were invited to New York to stay with relatives. My sister and I started our journey from Liverpool, on a ship called Eastern Prince, in the middle of heavy bombing, so I was told later on. We were, however, seemingly oblivious of danger. What I can remember was the fun we had on board, a huge crowd of kids with plenty of exciting activities, all unaware that we were the last children to make that transatlantic journey. The ship just in front of us, the *City of Benares*, was torpedoed and almost all the people on board were lost.

It was quite a change to live in a rather luxurious apartment on Park Avenue, not that the home life there was all that happy. We were lucky enough, however, to get a scholarship to a wonderful school. Now in its 100th year, Nightingale was, and still is, exceptional. Latin was a subject taught by a gentle scholar in a way that has lasted all my life. A teacher from France taught us French so accent became as important as having an extensive vocabulary, maths was made fascinating and so on. I excelled, made the honour board each year and even skipped a grade. The only lesson that I neither enjoyed nor was any good at was art. I think that the tensions of those years somewhat stifled any artistic activity. As it happened those were the only three years of proper education I received. Later, I realised that those years gave me the confidence to know that I was actually intelligent, creative and could achieve something. Just recently I found a quote that backed up this sentiment. In a book called *The End of Your Life Book Club*, by Will Schwalbe, talking about his mother he said: 'In the early 1950s she and her classmates were told something that no generation of women prior to theirs had ever heard, and by the Headmistress herself: that they could do anything and be anything – and have a husband and children to boot'. She had attended Brearley School. That is where, fitted with their green uniform, I would have gone had not Nightingale offered me a full scholarship. Both those schools were way ahead of their time.

All this confidence was completely obliterated by the depressing treatment I received on returning home. My parents quite rightly reasoned that, after the main dangers of invasion had passed, we should return home. Otherwise we would become too alienated from our own generation. In time for the assault of the Doodlebugs and V2s, we sailed back in a battered banana boat from New Orleans to Lisbon, and after various adventures and delays, we eventually flew back to England. The first

THE NIGHTINGALE-BAMFORD SCHOOL
20 EAST NINETY-SECOND STREET

Report of ROSEMARY WALEY

For January 28 - June 3, 1943

Rosemary is promoted to Class Vlll.

ATTENDANCE: Ex. Absence 8   Ex. Lateness 0   DEPORTMENT

Unex. Absence 0   Unex. Lateness 0

		Term	Examination
ENGLISH	Rosemary is able and intelligent. She has done a fine year's work. M.E.	A-	A
GRAMMAR		A	A+
SPELLING			A
FRENCH	Rosemary's work is excellent. Her pronunciation is good and her work is always well prepared. She is very eager to learn. L.S.	A	B+
ARITHMETIC	Rosemary's work is excellent. She is learning to restrain her desire to talk. S.Y.K.	A	A
SCIENCE	Rosemary does good work and has a thorough understanding of her Science. S.W.E.	B+	A
HISTORY	Rosemary does consistently good work. Intelligent grasp of essentials. E.H.	A-	A
GEOGRAPHY	Rosemary is an excellent student. She has a fine memory. M.E.	A-	A-
ART	Rosemary has great technical facility but is a little lazy about doing original work. H.F.	B	
CRAFTS	Rosemary has increasing skill in the use of her hands. H.F.	B+	
PHYSICAL EDUCATION	Rosemary has made excellent progress this year, but she must still guard against over-eagerness. D.W.	B	
MUSIC		B+	
SEWING	Excellent	A	
STUDY	Rosemary has excellent work habits.	A	

Rosemary was never late throughout the year.

Academic Honour Roll every report period this year.

THE Honour Roll for both report periods since the new report system was adopted.

Honourable Mention for High Average in Daily Work and in the Examinations in the Middle School.

	October	May
Height	5' ½"	5' 2½"
Weight	91 lbs.	100 lbs.

Louise H. Williard
CLASS TEACHER

Maya Stevenson Bamford
HEAD MISTRESS

My report card from Nightingale Bamford School, New York, as it was called then, dated 1943.
Note that my lowest mark, other than for physical education, was for art.

delay was caused by my sister catching measles, or was it chicken pox, while we were staying in a rather smart hotel in Estoril. Then a plane was shot down on the same route we were using to fly back to England. Because a famous actor was on board it got a lot of publicity, and caused more worry and more delay.

In my old school, both staff and students had had a difficult war. In retrospect, I can excuse what happened. However, all that I knew was derided and ignored. I knew the wrong things, all about Aztecs and Incas, but not the wives of Henry the Eighth. Long division of pounds, shillings and pence was a problem. The worst deprivation was that I was stopped abruptly from studying any science. I was judged to be too dangerous to be in the laboratory, as I supposedly did not know their rules. Luckily in those days I had a very good memory. All I could do was to memorise the curriculum and pass the necessary exams, in this case matriculation, at the age of fifteen. The basic examination was the School Certificate. To matriculate it was necessary to take certain special subjects and to achieve either distinction or credit in every one. The only problem was my banishment from the laboratory, but luckily geography came to the rescue, being classified somehow as a science, one of the essential subjects. Before the previous year and the passing of the 1945 Education Act, that would have been enough for university entrance.

My refuge was the art room. The new teacher, Margaret Gash, was gentle and understanding, very different from the rest of the staff. I could retreat and draw flowers, or better still learn lettering, which was one of her skills. Her influence on my life was incalculable, and we remained friends until she died recently, aged 99. It is amazing what you can do if you have to, and after two years, aged fifteen, almost the only subject I did not get a distinction for in my matriculation was art. Evidently my design for a headscarf did not impress the examiners.

My parents did not agree with university education for girls, but had I gone it would probably have been to study languages, because they were my strongest subject, and what career would that eventually have led to? However, when the time came to escape from school, the only thing that I could think of was to go to art school. It was not with any expectation of becoming an artist, but somehow it felt right. At the local art school I felt that finally I fitted in and it certainly turned out to be the right choice.

It led to a fascinating career that encompassed study and practice in several other unexpected areas. Opportunities arose in a series of lucky breaks and pure coincidences. Maybe the way such happenings are taken advantage of is influenced by one's nature, or maybe it was just that I had more than my share of good luck

Art school

It was just as well that I had no aspirations to be an artist, as at the local art school, the only qualification offered was the Art Teacher Diploma. This was also not what I wanted – I had already decided that I wanted to be a designer. From the early days I got little satisfaction either from lettering or flower painting unless the work was going to be used in some way, and not just put up on the wall. I was lucky in my main subject. Geoffrey Holden was a charismatic teacher, just graduated from the Royal College and a student of M C Oliver. I spent every possible moment in his weekly lettering classes. At the end of the year he said he had taught me all he could and suggested that I tried to go to his own teacher for further study. I was not the only person whose life he influenced. I noticed in later years that two of the mischievous young boys who caused so much havoc in his jewellery workshops, that I also joined, became owners of the two largest jewellers shops in the local town. Such is the power of a really good teacher.

I was not so lucky with textile classes. The girl who taught us had obviously never had any experience in the field. I remember her pouring scorn on a series of all-over abstract patterns that I produced. It was with huge satisfaction that all but one of those designs sold some years later to Liberty of Regent Street. Much needed life drawing classes were not much help either. On Mondays the teacher wore fancy waistcoats and a bow tie and he insisted that we all used 6h pencils and cross hatching for shading. On Fridays the other teacher made us use 6b pencils and our thumbs to shade the drawing. Between the two of them I never learned much about life drawing, but what I did learn was not to trust those who insisted on students copying their techniques (or to teach that way myself).

I probably dreamed of going on to another art school to continue my studies, most likely the Central School of Art (now Central Saint Martins). In retrospect it is just as well that this did not happen, because the practical experience that I obtained better suited me, and my aspirations to be a designer. This has made me consider whether an art school, or a university art degree as it has now become, is the best route for everyone. I have met several young people recently whose creativity has been stifled by such courses. They knew just what they wanted to do, and might have done better with a placement in a studio, or an apprenticeship. This leads me to question that creativity can certainly be stifled, but can it actually be taught?

Textile designing

After one year at art school my parents pronounced that I should get a job to show that I could not support myself with my ridiculous idea of being a designer. I could not, and still cannot, think of any better motivation to succeed than to prove them wrong. Sometimes I feel that I am still doing just that long after they have gone. Luckily a family friend knew of a textile design studio needing staff so, armed with my rather pitiful portfolio, I went for an interview. Haward studio was situated in Turnham Green, in south-west London near Chiswick, and had obviously been quite important in the past, judging by the examples on the walls. However, the studio had been left to relatives who knew little about the business. Anyhow, the chief designer was Sanderson trained, and he was in charge, which was all that mattered. I soon realised that what they wanted was cheap labour under the pretence that they were providing a good training. Well, I suppose that was so, but I soon negotiated a day a week to continue my lettering studies, which was just as well considering what happened later on. I have described the way we worked in the days before computers and even photographic colour separation, in *Textile Designing in the Mid 20th Century* published by the Book Guild.

Back at the studio we learned a lot from repeating the older designers' work, and there was always plenty more to do such as grinding and matching the body colours for finished drawings. Even so, there was enough time left for us to produce our own water colour sketches, working with our mahl sticks, standing up at our easels. There were three of us, working in the attic of the old red brick house. Though neither of the other girls had had any training they had already worked out their specialities. I chose mostly floral subjects to design to start with. Luckily we often had to produce designs for woven fabrics, as well as printed ones, in view of what happened some ten years later. While travelling home for over an hour on the underground and then the railway I would dream up ideas for designs and colour schemes.

Our sketches were taken away, presumably shown to clients, and that was the last we saw of them. It was exciting to hear that one of ours had been chosen, however, we were not allowed to do our own finished drawings. The chief designer took over from that stage onwards. Presumably he could alter our work if he or the client wished. During the three years that I worked there I never saw any finished product. Designers were not considered important in those days.

The central part of one of my floral sketches illustrating how detailed the work had to be before the days of photographic colour separation.

More lettering

I must not forget my important day off on Mondays. They started off with a visit to the Royal School of Needlework where I had found an opportunity for some work altering their needlework and tapestry designs to fit the needs of their clients. Tapestry work was very popular in those days for elderly retired men as well as women, helped by the publicity for Queen Mary's carpet. Then it was up to Hampstead Garden Suburb Institute where Mr Oliver, as we called him, held his classes. Here our letterforms were modified to match exactly those of our master.

Just after the war there were many memorial books and other demands for formal lettering, and the craft was very much alive. The word calligraphy was not used. Occasionally, we were allowed to join in some of this work. It was a rigorous scribal training in which we took much pride. When we were deemed to be of sufficiently

Mr Oliver's suggestions for an ampersand. They were written on the side of my work when I was designing a family tree.

high standard we would be put forward for membership of the Society of Scribes. Another student, Barbara, and I had our work sent to someone at the British Museum for our vellum to be stretched and mounted ready for the next meeting. However, in the meantime, Mr Oliver's daughter, Joyce, was put up for membership of the scribes, but she was blackballed by the committee. I use that word on purpose because there was no question that she, already an accomplished scribe, was not qualified. It must have been a political decision by the ladies of the committee. Barbara and I were so outraged that we removed our application and neither of us ever regretted it. They got their own back on me years later, but it served as a warning to me to be wary of committees that thought more of their own self-interest than the good of their craft.

Later on I felt that the strict method of training that we had followed had been rather limiting. What it did, however, was emphasize all the elements that affected your final work such as the way you sat, held the pen or different instrument, relaxed, or managed to get your paper in the optimum position. We worked on a slanting board and the paper was not fastened to it, but held by a loose band so that it could be moved as you progressed down the page. All these elements affected the quality of your work and became second nature. A letterer understands the practical factors involved in producing an efficient writing movement. From historical studies, we learned the delicate relationship between pen hold, tool and model. This knowledge became useful later on in the educational and medical world where a trained eye is needed to detect movement faults, as well as an open mind to detect those problems that are letterform orientated, and those caused by tension either of hand or mind.

After three enjoyable years there came the day when we were all summoned to the office and told that the studio was closing. We were given a week's wages. In my case it was just three pounds, and that was that. The problem was what to do next, whether to stay with textile designing or try a scribal career. There were three of us called Rosemary in the lettering class. One went on to the College of Heralds, and the other one went to do ticket writing for the well-known store, Heals. Neither of these jobs would have appealed to me. In those days the work of a scribe was still that of a very traditional craft. In my rather empty teenage years I had craved uniformity and revelled in the joy of following and copying my master's script. I realised, luckily in time, that I was not sufficiently a perfectionist, and that with so little opportunity to be creative, it was not the ideal full-time career for me, much though I enjoyed it.

I decided to try freelance designing, not realising that it was a slump in the textile trade that had forced our studio to close. It was very satisfying producing my own collection, and having so much freedom to choose subject and style. I sold quite a few, including the ones to Liberty's, but usually it was then a matter of 'come back in six months time'. It was pretty obvious I would not be able to support myself this way and unfortunately, in the uncertain post-war days, that was the most important thing. The dreaded secretarial course, threatened by my parents, loomed dangerously close. In despair I spent the last of my savings (mostly the result of lettering commissions done at weekends and the freelance work I did for the Royal School of Needlework) on a holiday. What happened next was the first of the coincidences that changed the course of my life. On the train to Dover I picked up a discarded newspaper, the *Daily Telegraph* if I remember correctly. In it I spotted an advertisement. It said, 'wanted a designer who is good at lettering and has studio experience'. This sounded like the ideal job for me, and it was.

Packaging design

The studio was part of *Waxed Papers Ltd*, then a flourishing firm devoted to producing packaging of all kinds for food, and other commodities. This might sound rather unexciting but it was a works studio. We could see our designs go through all the stages from sketch, to customer approval, to printing blocks to seeing them coming out on the machines and eventually in the shops. This could be exhilarating. In addition, learning about all the production techniques was so important.

In later years, as expensive design companies started up, it was evident that either they did not know, or they did not care, how their designs would be produced. This was no part of their experience or job description. I am not suggesting that the designs that they presented to their clients were anything other than beautiful. They were beautiful, but they did not take printing methods into consideration. Customers came to us with fabulously complex designs that they wanted produced in the cheapest possible way. To be successfully reproduced they would need to be printed by the most expensive method, photogravure. They blamed us when using what I think was termed flexographic, but we called rubber printing – which was all they could afford – proved unsatisfactory. It left me with a certain distrust of this kind of design marketing.

Classical lettering proved to be an advantage in the studio. It was 1952, with the coronation coming up. Heraldry and royal decoration had to be on everything from penny chocolate bars on to much more expensive items. Later on quite different kinds

Working at my slanting desk at the packaging studio.

Classical designs were very useful leading up to the coronation, but later much more informal and modern lettering was needed.

of letterforms were required. Our job was to make a product desirable in the eyes of the purchaser and uphold the brand of the producer (although such terms were seldom heard in those days). More simply, it was to present the product in such a way that it would stand out in any display, and through design, colour and individualized letterforms, tempt the shopper into buying it. In other words, the manufacturer was the client, and our job was to attract, and sometimes deceive, the customer. I remember discovering that the most expensive shop in London purchased its confectionery from the cheapest manufacturer. We had to make it all look as opulent and extravagant as possible. The fun (or skill) was to invent letters to suit every product, although there

CONTRACTORS TO — THE WAR OFFICE

TAVENER RUTLEDGE

HENRY TAVENER (MANAGING) W.N.TOD, A.J.TAVENER **LIMITED** W.N.McQUEEN (SECRETARY) J.S.TAVENER, W.H.TAVENER

TELEPHONE: ANFIELD 3451 (3 LINES)

TELEGRAMS: "ECLAIR LIVERPOOL 7"

YOUR REF   OUR REF

HYT/ES

Olde English Taveners FRUIT DROPS

The Sweetest Sweet

BEECH STREET EDGE LANE

LIVERPOOL · 7

DATE

Friday: 1st November, 1957

Miss R. Waley,
Messrs. Waxed-Papers Limited,
Nunhead Lane,
London, S.E.15.

Dear Miss Waley,

       Having received the two panel design wrappers and subjected them to normal factory procedure I would like you to know that your designs have met with full approval and in fact acclamation, and not only are a very big improvement on our present design but open the door to new productions. May we just say many thanks.

       Yours faithfully,
       TAVENER RUTLEDGE LTD.

       Henry Tavener.

P.S. Your design outstrips our label.
A few are enclosed, have you any
ideas, or perhaps this is not
your department?

A somewhat over enthusiastic reaction to a
five-minute sketch. The word 'Taveners' was
not my work.

Taveners

THE ORIGINAL
CHOCOLATE
ECLAIRS
HAND DIPPED

8ᴰ

were a few display types around. It may sound strange but I developed a technique of sinking myself in the product to feel what it was like. I used this same technique in later years to feel what it was like to be a patient with complex problems.

In the early days the studio equipment was pretty basic, but as the importance of design became more recognised, a new and better-equipped studio was built. As my experience and perhaps confidence in my abilities also grew, I had an idea. It was quite revolutionary at the time, at least outside of London. We had previously been dependent on the firm's travelling salesmen or so-called representatives, to relay the customer's ideas for design. This was not very satisfactory. I thought it would be better for me to travel to see clients to discuss their needs, and this was agreed. I used to set out by rail, equipped so that I could listen to their views, produce a quick sketch and then wrap it around their product. Sometimes I gave them ideas for how to display their goods, or quick ideas for a new logo. It worked well, from South Wales to Liverpool and even more distant, I had fun, but there was one serious problem. There were no copyright laws, so there was nothing to stop a firm from giving us the initial order and then using my ideas to switch to a cheaper manufacturer.

After nearly seven years our benevolent studio manager, Mr Ralston, came up from his home on the south coast less and less often. I was left to deal with all the everyday problems, from deciding who designed what, to ordering printing blocks, and keeping a rebellious staff in order. I was not good at what could be called 'man management'. There was also talk of the firm being taken over by a larger company. I felt it was time for a change. I saw an advertisement from the prestigious Design Research Unit and went for an interview. They seemed pleased to have someone with practical experience but asked me to come back in a couple of months as they were enlarging their studio. Searching for something to do in the meantime, I applied for quite a different temporary job. The position was for a designer who could speak several languages, which luckily I could. It was to man (if that is the right word) the British design exhibit at the 1958 Brussels World Fair. I went to the interview and got the post mostly, I imagine, on the strength of my languages. Off I went to be fitted for my uniform by the prestigious designer, Norman Hartnell, only to get engaged that very evening. I eventually landed up in Uganda instead of Brussels.

THE COUNCIL OF INDUSTRIAL DESIGN

THE DESIGN CENTRE

28 Haymarket, London S.W.1 · Telephone TRAfalgar 8000

Personal
J.O'N/KMB

1st February, 1958

Dear Miss Waley,

   With further reference to your application for the
post of Receptionist/Display Assistant on the staff of
the Council, I should be glad if you would come here for
a shortlist interview at 10.30 a.m. on Thursday, 6th
February, to meet our Chief Exhibitions' Officer,
Mr. P. I. Fellows, and Major-General J. M. Benoy, who is
in charge of our reception staff.

   Will you please ask for me when you arrive.

                              Yours sincerely,

                              Barford.

                              Secretary to
                              Mrs. J. O'Neilly
                              Administration Division

Miss R. Waley,
Wavertree,
Mt. Harry Road,
Sevenoaks,
Kent .

A letter from the Council of Industrial Design. It concerned a job at the Brussels World Fair. I was offered it but did not take up the post, going to Africa instead.

MAKERERE COLLEGE

FROM THE SECRETARY
A. TATTERSALL, M.A.

P. O. BOX 262
KAMPALA. UGANDA.

TELEPHONE: KAMPALA 2471

THE UNIVERSITY COLLEGE OF EAST AFRICA

March 14th, 1961.

Mrs. J.P. Sassoon,
P.O. Box 263,
KAMPALA.

Dear Mrs. Sassoon,

I write on behalf of the Council of Makerere College, The University College of East Africa, to offer you a part-time appointment in our School of Fine Art, with effect from the commencement of our next Academic Year, on 17th July, 1961.

The appointment consists of two three-hour sessions per week, the actual days to be arranged between Professor Todd and yourself. The duties of the appointment will be to lecture in lettering, typography and allied subjects. The salary offered is at the rate of £6.6.0 per session.

The appointment would not entitle you to any paid leave.

I understand that you may not be able to commence work until later in the year. I should be glad if you would let me know whether you can accept this offer, and if so, when you will be free to commence your duties. Also, if you would let the Bursar know the name of the Bank and the designation of the account into which your salary should be paid. I am also asking Professor Todd, by copy of this letter, to inform the Bursar each month of the number of sessions which you have worked.

Yours sincerely,

SECRETARY,
MAKERERE COLLEGE COUNCIL.

A letter from Makerere College, part of The University of East Africa. It offered me a post in the department of fine art.

Less productive years

I sometimes think of my mother-in-law whom I never met. She died just after the war from some undiagnosed complaint. I have always thought probably the war itself had a lot to do with it. She had three sons. The eldest, in the army, was captured in Italy and spent the rest several years in a prisoner of war camp. Her second son was in the air force and was killed in a raid over Germany, then her youngest, my eventual husband, was sent to Burma. As it happened, hostilities were nearly over by then, but I wonder whether he would have survived that particularly brutal war if the atom bomb had not been dropped.

After his war service and university my husband had declined all the offers from family businesses and decided on a career in education. He had already had three exciting years working in Uganda before we met. To give an idea of what was expected of him, early on he had been allocated a plot of land and told to build a secondary school, which he did somehow. He started it off and then handed it over to a permanent head, and went back to the capital, Kampala. I wonder if anything was as much fun again.

With three moves in three years and two babies there was not much time for me to work during my stay in Africa. I enjoyed the time there so much – the people, the country and everything – and I would have loved to stay longer. All I have to remind me of work from that time is a logo I designed for the Uganda Electricity Board. Just before we left on leave, I was offered an exciting post. It was in the School of Fine Art at Makerere College, part of the University of East Africa. It was supposed to teach lettering, typography and allied subjects which I understood to include textile designing. I went in to the department several times and realised what a wonderful opportunity it would be. I would have been working with that fascinating man (young man then) Jonathan Kingdon. Back to England I started planning, but it was not to be. With Uganda near to independence everyone was encouraged to find careers back in the UK. It might have been a disaster anyhow as I rather feel that that particular task was beyond me at that stage.

Textiles again

My husband's work as an education officer took us to Bradford, in Yorkshire. Rather bored, I was listening to the radio one day when I heard that wonderful textile designer, Lucienne Day, whose work I had always admired, deploring the lack of designers of woven fabrics. Until then I had not thought of reverting to textile designing, but hastily scanning the local paper, there were several interesting advertisements for designers for the Jacquard industry, as it was called.

I started working for a traditional firm who only wanted single motifs to be repeated by their untrained employees. It was not much fun but it suited a busy mother with two small children. I soon found better clients, among them the Fletcher brothers, who ran several linked mills near Keithley. Lucienne Day was quite right. They had to import from Germany, beautifully finished but very expensive designs for their woven fabrics. Together with their chief designer we devised a method that allowed them to work from my black and white, dry brush and half tone designs. These were quick to produce and allowed them to have much less expensive designs and a freer choice more suited to their needs. There were many other mills as well whose directors, although they were surprised to find a woman on their doorstep, most unusual in those days, were extremely pleasant to work with. Eventually, I persuaded Fletcher's to have six monthly or annual collections, like the fashion trade, quite revolutionary at that time. Those years, and the now almost vanished Jacquard trade are recorded in *Designing Textiles in the Mid 20th Century*.

By now we had moved back to the south of England, and as the travel became more tedious, I decided to revert to my other skill, lettering. However, not everything in life goes according to plan. On a holiday in Norway, our youngest daughter suffered a tick bite. She developed encephalitis and was ill for a couple of years and finally ended up in Great Ormond Street Hospital. Parents were chucked out of the wards after lunch to allow the children to rest. One day I took refuge in the library of The Central School (now Central Saint Martin's) that was just around the corner. I felt at home as it was there that I used to attend evening classes there with Mr Oliver many years before. Nicolete Gray, that great expert in all aspects of letterforms, approached me. She wanted to know what I was doing in 'her' library. After I explained the situation and what I did she could not have been kinder. At that time I was very much isolated from others in my profession. Her suggestion was that I should apply to join a group of those interested in letterforms. It met a couple of times a year in the Department of Typography and Graphic Communication at the University of Reading. I was not

C. H. Fletcher Ltd.

Manufacturers of Rayon Brocades for Furnishings, Dress Goods, etc.

EST. 1903.

DIRECTORS:
W. K. FLETCHER.
G. S. FLETCHER.
P. FLETCHER.
W. D. R. FLETCHER, M.SC.TECH.

Airedale Shed,
Silsden
Yorkshire.

ALSO AT
WOODLANDS MILL, STEETON.
TEL. STEETON 2312.

TELEPHONE : STEETON 2274-5.   TELEGRAMS : "VIGOR, SILSDEN"

OUR REF.   YOUR REF.

NS/JM

9th April, 1964.

Mrs. J. P. Sassoon,
12 Woodlands Grove,
BAILDON.

Dear Mrs. Sassoon,

Further to your visit on Tuesday the 14th April, we enclose herewith a range of designs that we have produced on both the Dress and Furnishings. We should like you to examine these patterns and return them to us at some later date and we would also remind you that the maximum size of repeat on the Dress looms is 6", of which we run both single shuttle illustrated in one colour of weft and pick/pick which is illustrated in two colour wefts. On the Furnishing cloths we can use either 6" or 12" repeat on the single shuttle stripes whereas on the multi-coloured pick/pick designs our repeat is 6". This particular cloth the pick/pick multi-weft cloth is illustrated at the bottom of the furnishing swatch. The designs on this particular particular quality have been mainly traditional designs as this is a more expensive cloth. On the stripes and solid colour Spun Viscose warps where our repeats can be 6" or 12" the writer showed you one or two sketches that we were developing at present and these designs can be of an abstract or modern floral design.

There is no hurry in returning the swatches of designs we are enclosing but we should like them back at some later date.

If you would like to submit any ideas that you are working on in the rough state we should be pleased to pass our opinion on these in order that you are working on the right lines for us.

Yours faithfully,
Per pro. C.H. Fletcher Ltd.

Enclosure

A letter from C H Fletcher Ltd concerning designs for the textile trade. I worked for them for several years.

able to attend for quite a while but in the end this had a tremendous effect on my life, and I have always been grateful to her.

Lettering as a decorative art

It was Prince Philip who provided the impetus for my next step. It was reported in the press that he had criticised the standard of goods produced for sale to the tourist trade. This suggested there might be an opportunity for lettered material that combined something decorative with a relevant message. In other words using calligraphy, as it was now widely called, as a decorative art. I wondered if I would be accused of prostituting my craft and consulted the great David Kindersley whom I met by chance at an exhibition. He was kind enough not to laugh at me and encouraged me instead. We later became good friends. At first I took original pieces to the various expensive gift shops that targeted tourists, but soon decided that printed material was the way forward.

I remember that I first took my ideas to the London store, John Lewis, where I was directed to the gift buyer. He was looking for an exclusive set of tablemats. At that time the company that they sourced their mats from was called Lady Clare. Their most popular design was based on the wrought iron gates of Lady Clare's own stately home. They were the work of the famous designer Tigou. The imaginative and friendly buyer

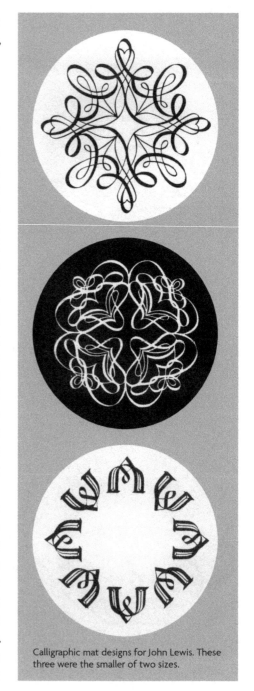

Calligraphic mat designs for John Lewis. These three were the smaller of two sizes.

30

considered that a calligraphic pattern would work just as well for their clients. It was one of my most enjoyable but difficult commissions, and resulted in six large and six small mats. Then I visited Harrods and they wanted some mats based on ancient recipes. Mats based on herbals were ordered from another company, and so it went on. I visited the local printers, Salmons, and the result was five years of recipe calendars. Recipes for textiles and packaging etc all needed new material. To start with I sourced this from ancient recipe books and herbals in the British Museum. In those days I was able to access the originals, and copy what I wanted – without even having to wear protective gloves.

Running short of material one day I went to my local public library. There I found an amazing book, *The Delectable Past* written by Esther Aresty, an American, who apparently had the largest private collection of ancient recipe books. Her material was extremely useful and I was very grateful but felt rather guilty about using so many her recipes without permission. I did something that I had never done before, and wrote to her including an example of one of her recipes that I had lettered and illustrated. That unexpectedly, prompted the next step in my career.

My first book

Rather disappointed by having had no reply from Esther, I was pleasantly surprised by a phone call from her some time later, from London. I invited her down for lunch and was in such a state that the pastry for the planned smoked salmon tart did not work out, and it all ended up as scrambled eggs (with the salmon) on toast. She had arrived with an offer from her editor at the publisher Simon and Schuster, for me to write a book on calligraphy. I had kept all my old work and probably had, at the back of my mind an idea that it would all make a book sometime, but would not have known how to start. This was the just what I needed. I began to put things together but it was not to be. Sadly the editor suddenly died. It would have been difficult anyhow, inexperienced as I was, to deal with a publisher the other side of the Atlantic in the days before emails and scanners.

Help came from an unexpected source. I had a request from Robert Graves' literary agent to letter one of his poems as a presentation piece. It was one of my favourite lettering commissions. When he came to collect it I took the opportunity of asking him how one went about finding an agent. Rather to my surprise he said something that proved absolutely true, that I would never need an agent. He gave me the name of an elderly publisher who seemed very enthusiastic about my idea. At the time I had only told one person of my plans – Dorothy Mahoney, the well known scribe, who lived nearby and was a good friend. She rang me a few days after my visit to the publisher, in a great state of excitement. She said that she had been commissioned to write a book on calligraphy but added that it sounded just like mine. She was quite correct. It was my idea and my publisher had sent my book to be reviewed by the secretary of the Society of Scribes. She had a long memory (I had better not mention her name) and apparently had said 'do not have her, she is not a member, have someone who is'. Dorothy was appalled but there was nothing to be done. She wrote a marvellous book, *The Craft of Calligraphy,* but shortly afterwards that particular publisher went out of business. Luckily her book was taken up later and published by The Pelham Press.

That unpleasant experience might have put me off writing for life. It certainly confirmed my distrust of closed societies. Fortunately my book found a very happy home with Thames and Hudson, shortly to be followed by three more that I wrote for them. Incidentally, as they were the first paperbacks published by them, initially I only received half the usual royalties. I think that the success of that first book was that it was directed at the general public. Previous books, written by celebrated calligraphers, had all been directed at professionals – or at any rate were of a very high standard. From the start I wanted my craft to be available to anyone, and decided on evolving a much simpler and less strict method of teaching. I suggested starting with double pencils and pattern, to get used to the angle, and then on to stroke-related families of letters and finally ink.

Anyhow, *The Practical Guide to Calligraphy* stayed in print for over twenty years and sold countless thousands, many to American book clubs. Even when it was out of print an American company that sold craft materials ordered another eighty-five thousand copies. I wonder if there are many moments as exciting as when you get the first copy of your first book in your hands, of course other than your first baby. Some years later I wrote a sequel, *Lettering From Formal to Informal,* starting in rather the same way, but continuing on to illustrate how much I had progressed to teaching informal rather than classic lettering. Esther Aresty had also given me some good advice. She said that once I started to write I would never be happy finishing one book without having plans for the next one. How right she was, I went on to have a book published almost every year for over 30 years.

Teaching lettering

As I was writing a book promoting a more relaxed way of learning lettering, I thought it would be a good idea to test out my method. An old school friend had been asked to start the first adult education calligraphy classes in our part of the country. She already had a full time job so asked me, just at the right time, to take them on. My classes were a mixture from young designers from the local publisher, Hodder and Stoughton, to elderly bereaved ladies just wanting some new occupation. I taught on a one-to-one basis, encouraging the hesitant and pushing those more competent on to a higher level. All went well and really imaginative, and sometimes quite competent work was produced, until the incompetent and pompous head of the centre intervened. He announced that my method of teaching one-to-one was wasteful, and that I must conduct all classes from the front of the class in future. Moreover, I should attend a course that he was about to run on how to teach. After two years it was time for me to leave! There was one final result of this enterprise. Just as I was leaving I got a call from someone at our local education authority, Kent. They said, as I was teaching calligraphy (as they interpreted it) would I now teach teachers how to deal with handwriting problems in schools?

Part 2

Changing direction

Handwriting in schools

At first I said that handwriting was not really my subject. Anyhow, I did not want to take the project on, my lettering and design work was taking off and I was getting more and more interesting commissions. It certainly was not an area that I was particularly interested in at the time. I said that I would try and find someone else to take on the training of teachers but no one was interested. There was probably no money in it and no prestige attached to the subject. At that time, at the peak of the italic fashion, the money (and let's be honest) the ego was in producing copybooks. Some were good but some were awful. Your handwriting is a reflection of yourself on paper and it must have been very satisfying, if you had a particularly beautiful script, to think that children all over the country would be taught in your style.

However it did not always work out so successfully. The copybooks completely ignored the fact that there was no special training for the teachers, and italic writing, in particular, had its own problems for the uninformed. For instance, I am not a natural italic writer but had to learn the script for professional work. I was aware, for example, that to be successful you had to make sure that your hand was placed slightly on edge, as many artists' hands do when they work, not almost flat on the writing surface, probably how the majority of children would write. There were many unfortunate consequences, such as slow, jagged interpretations of the model. I should add here that later on when I was asked to judge an annual national handwriting competition there were some enviably beautiful examples of italic handwriting from schools where experts had taught the pupils. It was always difficult not to award them all the prizes!

I already had some experience of the result of the poor teaching of the subject. We had three daughters at a school where italic handwriting was badly taught. My eldest daughter was a prolific writer but never could master a fast enough italic to keep up with her thoughts. She was castigated on the grounds of her handwriting, that it did not conform to the school model. The next daughter adopted a slow, rather jagged italic. She was not praised for that, only criticised for not producing lengthy essays like her sister. By the time the third daughter came along I think they had given up, and all three went on to develop a fast, flowing natural hand, that has served them well, with no trace of italic in it. In retrospect the knowledge that I had absorbed through my scribal training was much more than I realised. I explained this in the *Art and Science of Handwriting*: 'this meant that I knew letters, not only from the visual outside, but from the inside. A scribe can look at a letter and see as well as feel how it was written – where it starts, and which way it proceeds, where the pressures are and above all whether the writer was tense or relaxed'.

I tried to find anything serious written about actual handwriting problems, but there was nothing to be found. In the end I reluctantly decided the only thing to do was to accept the challenge. I never thought that this subject would take up so much of my time for the next 25 years, but what I found was a complete vacuum. Although there obviously were serious problems no one seemed to care. In all probability no one had the knowledge, or was willing to give the time to sort things out. The question for me was where to start? In those days there was a teachers' centre in each town that dealt with problems of literacy in local schools. There were not any special needs teachers in individual schools. The local centre seemed as good a place as any to begin my investigation. The head teacher there suggested that I looked at two primary schools, one that was considered the worst and one the best in the district.

The worst was indescribable. A Catholic school, handwriting was certainly not one of its priorities. No one seemed alarmed or even faintly interested by the obvious problems. The best was a delightful school perched high on a hill in an outlying village. My first impression there, even before I looked closely at any script, was of pain. The children's bodies were twisted in odd positions as they sat to work, their hands likewise. As for their simple print, it looked fairly legible at first sight, but looking closer their letters were seldom formed correctly. The teachers seemed to have no idea of the importance of the ductus of letters. That term refers to the point of entry and direction of strokes involved in the writing of individual letters. There seemed to be no recognition, to put it simply, that letters should start at the right place and proceed in the correct direction. The teachers did not notice or seem to mind about how letters were formed as long as they could read what was written. If they were ever going to progress towards a joined-up script those children were going to have a lot of trouble. In neither school was there any evidence of a model or other teaching material. All was dependent on the individual teacher's script and their only worry, other than if the writing was legible, was whether pupils had a conventional pen hold.

The unconventional ways that the children held their pens worried them. If they had known any history they would have understood that every time a new writing implement was invented, such as a metal pen after a quill, a change of pen hold was recommended. What has happened in the last half century is that now children start to mark-make with felt pens, not coloured pencils. When using pencils they might easily have learned a conventional pen hold. From felt pens to biros, modern implements function quite differently. They need to be held in a more upright position to make them work. This requires different pressures from the fingers so that usually an unconventional hold becomes automated early on. This still is not understood today, with a conventional pen hold illustrated in every handwriting manual, and pupils being chastised for not conforming.

The only conclusion that I could come to – not initially, but after several years of observing pupils as they got older, was this: that if an unconventional pen hold was working for a pupil, did not cause them pain, enabled them to make all the necessary strokes involved in letters and did not slow them down then it was advisable to let things alone because it is incredibly difficult for a pupils to alter an automated pen hold. The best motivation for change was if it caused pain. The special needs teachers hopefully could deal with reading or spelling difficulties but not when it came to handwriting problems. Too often any strategy was directed towards trying to intervene with a child's style of writing. In some cases the arbitrarily chosen model could itself be the cause of a pupil's trouble. There was no understanding that with a clear diagnosis, encouragement and praise, rather than uninformed criticism, pupils, particularly those past the very early stages, could often find their own solutions. I always tried to explain the damage done by constant criticism but in the early days there was no course of training to follow. It was not much use to say that an understanding of all the issues involved could only come from close observation and an open mind.

When I went into secondary schools the problems were even more pronounced. A whole generation of teenagers were not equipped with a script adequate for their

Unconventional pen holds – left hand

Left-handers try to solve their special problems, but do not always succeed.

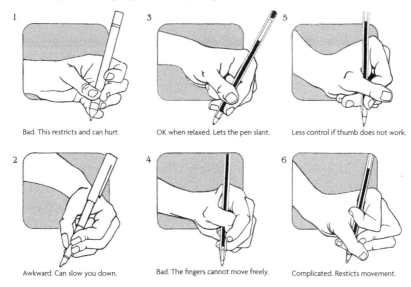

1   Bad. This restricts and can hurt.

3   OK when relaxed. Lets the pen slant.

5   Less control if thumb does not work.

2   Awkward. Can slow you down.

4   Bad. The fingers cannot move freely.

6   Complicated. Resticts movement.

Unconventional pen holds – right hand

You need to try out these pen holds to feel why some work and others do not.

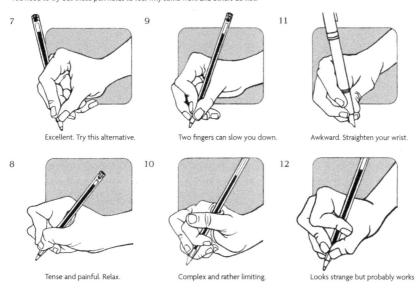

7   Excellent. Try this alternative.

9   Two fingers can slow you down.

11   Awkward. Straighten your wrist.

8   Tense and painful. Relax.

10   Complex and rather limiting.

12   Looks strange but probably works

Unconventional pen holds, both right handed and left handed. Note the upright angle of the pens, also number 7, the alternate pen hold. Illustrations from *Handwriting Problems in the Secondary School*.

needs as they got older and had to deal with external examinations. This, of course, was before the general use of computers in schools, but even now examinations need to be handwritten. The most serious condition that I found was the prevalence of pain and tension in their hands. In severe cases this could stop pupils from being able to write at all. Something was desperately needed and all I could think of was to write a book

My first handwriting book

When I now look at *The Practical Guide to Children's Handwriting*, originally published in 1983, though I knew much less than I know now there is not so much that I would alter, just quite a lot that I might add. Both a simple teaching method and ways of dealing with the most common problems were what were needed at that time. Many copybooks taught letters in alphabetical order where the letters that followed

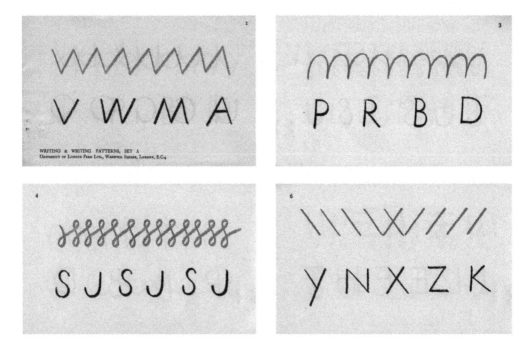

Illustrations from set B of small booklets, part of Marion Richardson's *Writing & Writing Patterns*. Reproduced from *Marion Richardson, Her life and her Contribtion to Handwriting*.

each other bore no resemblance in terms of movement. I recommended starting with simple pattern and then progressing to letters in stroke related sequences. This was how I had taught my calligraphy students. In this way young children soon pick up, practise and automate the correct point of entry and direction of stroke. To me, this automation the movement of letters, the ductus, was of primary importance. Dr Maria Montessori had reiterated this in her memorable statement, 'learning handwriting is stocking the muscle memory'. As far as copybooks were concerned, this was also by no means original. Marion Richardson stressed the importance of dealing with letters in stroke related sequences. Her excellent method was described in detail in *Writing and Writing Patterns*. The University of London first published her teacher's book and five beautiful copybooks in 1935.

The reaction to the handwriting book surprised us all. It was reviewed everywhere from the *Times Educational Supplement* downwards. One amusing consequence was a request to appear on morning television with the popular Michael Buerk. The first part of the interview was relatively easy but then two problem children were produced out of the blue, and I was expected to diagnose and deal with their problems on air. I suppose it went all right because I remained in Broadcasting House for most of the day answering phone calls from worried parents and schools. After this everything just accelerated. Schools all over the country wanted in-service days, as well as whole districts asking for help. Individual parents and teachers contacted me with their problems. Their children came from all kinds of schools from small state primary schools to expensive pubic schools.

Problems with letterforms alone were usually fairly easy to deal with, however, not all were actual handwriting issues. I remember two cases in particular. One was a thirteen-year-old boy who was referred to me by an observant teacher. He was diagnosed as dyslexic and destined for a special school. This immediately raised doubts in me after hearing that his favourite subjects were history and English. I asked about sports. He answered that he hated all sports because he could never see the ball. A quick trip to the local orthoptist who prescribed the necessary glasses and his problem was solved and on he went happily, not to a special school for dyslexics, but to join his brother in his chosen public school. Worse still was a fifteen-year-old girl from a boarding school who was referred to as 'backward'. When I watched her trying to write, her eyes seemed to try to focus in an awkward way – difficult to explain other than to say she was not looking at her work in a way that seemed natural. Again the orthoptist solved her rather more complex problem. The letter she wrote afterwards to me said it all; 'if only someone had noticed this earlier how different my life would have been'. When I look back, quite a significant proportion of children referred to me suffered from an undiagnosed visual problem.

There were more serious cases sent by worried teachers or parents. Some of the handwriting samples indicated such severe tension that they prompted further enquiries about either home or school environment. It seemed to me that the only ethical way of dealing with the situation was to expose myself to as many different problems as possible and, incidentally, to never charge anyone. I felt it essential to learn as much as possible before I felt justified in making further recommendations. It was fairly frantic. All this time I was amassing hundreds of examples, photographs and other data, all of which was to be useful later on, and now is kept safely in the archives of the Institute of Education at London University.

Further developments

There was still not much recognition of the serious problems elsewhere. My eldest daughter was studying for a post-graduate qualification in special educational needs. She asked the head of department if he would like a talk on handwriting problems. The reply was something like, 'it is not relevant – but I would like some free books from her'. This course was one of the only ones in the country for those who would be responsible for pupils' special needs in the future – and handwriting problems were not considered relevant. She also sent me details of an international conference on the acquisition of symbolic skills. It was meant just for my interest and she was not expecting me to attend – but I applied and was accepted. It was my first time at a major international conference and I rather hesitantly produced a colourful poster display, designed with the help of my friend Gunnlauger Briem, who I had met at the letterform meetings at the University of Reading. It was based on some parts of the new book and caused somewhat of a stir. Believe it or not, in an international conference on the subject of graphic development, my work was almost the only mention of handwriting. Amazingly, I found both the call for papers and full programme after so many years.

So many things happened around this time that it is quite hard to be certain which came first. To begin with I had only dealt with children's problems, but adult worries soon crept in. The first person I can remember was someone with a debilitating neurological condition who lived locally. She had lost the ability to do what she

INTERNATIONAL CONFERENCE ON
THE ACQUISITION OF SYMBOLIC SKILLS
SPONSORED BY NATO

UNIVERSITY OF KEELE, ENGLAND
5th - 10 JULY, 1982

Organizing Committee:

P. Bryant, Oxford	R. Cromer, MRC London
D. Rogers, Keele	J. Sloboda, Keele

CALL FOR PAPERS AND REGISTRATIONS

The conference will be organized as a series of symposia with emphasis on:

MATHEMATICAL AND COMPUTING SKILLS
LOGICAL SKILLS IN CHILDREN
MUSICAL SKILLS
SYMBOLIC SKILLS IN THE DEAF
SPELLING AND HANDWRITING
DRAWING
MAP AND NAVIGATIONAL SKILLS
FIRST LANGUAGE ACQUISITION
SECOND LANGUAGE ACQUISITION

Principal Speakers:

U. Neisser, Cornell	U. Bellugi, Salk Institute
S. Farnham-Diggory, Delaware	P. Bryant, Oxford
W. G. Chase, Carnegie-Mellon	R. Cromer, MRC London
D. Deutsch, San Diego	U. Frith, MRC London
J. J. Goodnow, McQuarie	G. Hitch, Manchester
W. C. Ritchie, Syracuse	D. Wood, Nottingham

Abstracts (150 words) with summaries (1000 words) should be sent to D. Rogers or J. Sloboda, Department of Psychology, University of Keele, Keele, Staffs. ST5 5BG, England, by *1st January, 1982.* Speakers will be alloted 30 minutes, including question time. Papers should preferably be in English, since there will be no translation facilities.

The conference will be open to non-speaker participants, with a maximum attendance, including speakers, of 200. Early registration is advised, and no registration will be accepted after *1st May, 1982.*

The conference is likely to be of special interest to people working in Psychology, Linguistics or Education.

Keele University is set in parkland near to the Potteries Towns, where Wedgwood, Spode and Royal Doulton are situated. Excursions will be arranged to Chatsworth, Stratford on Avon and other places of local interest.

For further details write to:
The Conference Secretary
Acquisition of Symbolic Skills
Department of Psychology
University of Keele
Keele, Staffs. ST5 5BG
England
Telex: 36113 UNKLIB G

drawing →

Many of the names are familiar but having started to identify them with subject areas I realize I can't. Maybe Alan Wing could help?

The first conference that I attended. There were very few presentations or displays on the subject of handwriting, which was surprising considering the title of the conference, and mine got quite a lot of attention.

43

enjoyed most – writing notices for her church. She could no longer control her hand or wrist but her shoulder was seemed fine. I was able to show her how to write like Victorian scribes did - from the shoulder, keeping the hand still. History can be useful and at least for a while that would solve her problem.

Then came a case through the teacher network. A head mistress had damaged her right hand in an accident, permanently severing the tendons. She feared that she would never write again and risked losing her job. It seemed essential to train her to use her left hand. That is usually a very difficult job, and something I would not consider doing unless in severe circumstances such as this. It was surprisingly easy for her, with a new pen and pen hold, new paper position and a few different letterforms, to make it easier for a left-hander. Her colleagues soon said that they could read her writing better than before. It showed me how sheer desperation and motivation could overcome seemingly almost impossible difficulties. Anyhow, this had positive repercussions. She had a brother who worked for the publisher Hodder and Stoughton. He evidently heard about this, and knowing that the publisher was looking for someone to write a book about handwriting in the *Teach Yourself* series, came to me. This was going to be quite an arduous enterprise.

At this point it is quite difficult to separate all that was going on in my life into chronological order. I had met Briem, a letterer and designer. He was in the middle of producing a handwriting scheme for his native Iceland. Our ideas seem to coincide so we decided to tackle this project together. It taught me lot about how to design a book, and once again, *Teach Yourself Handwriting* was a success. What was initially a fairly modest volume in 1984 has been enlarged, renamed several times, and over thirty years later still sells several thousand worldwide annually, now renamed *Improve Your Handwriting*. Again it seems there is still an unfilled gap in the market. Incidentally, through Briem, I was invited to Iceland to talk about handwriting problems. It certainly is a fascinating country, and I only made one mistake, I asked about how they dealt with left-handed problems – the answer was 'we do not have any left-handed writers in Iceland'. I quickly changed the subject.

About this time an exciting prospect arose from another meeting of the letterform group at Reading. At one session the subject of calligraphy had come up and someone mentioned that nothing was being done nowadays in that area. I disagreed and therefore was asked to organise a meeting on that subject. The obvious speaker was my old friend from the days with Mr Oliver, Anne Camp. She had just started teaching a course at Roehampton College. What happened was that she gave an enthralling talk on the history of calligraphy, and in doing so used all of her half of the morning and most of my allotted time, as well. I do not think that the audience of experts would have been half as interested in what I had to say. There was just enough time for me to display the work of my students and demonstrate the simpler method of teaching that I was using. Then I made two statements. One was explaining how difficult it was to teach even a formal alphabet to pupils whose personal handwriting differed significantly from the model. Secondly, if an absolute beginner had never even picked up a broad edged pen it was relatively easy to teach them some good letters in a surprisingly short time. If, however, they had already played about by themselves they took a long time to get out of any bad habits before they could progress.

An introduction to the Medical Research Council

It certainly interested one member of the audience. I never asked Dr Alan Wing, then a senior psychologist at the Applied Psychology Unit of the Medical Research Council in Cambridge, how he came to be at the meeting. Anyhow, he came up to me saying that he found what I said most interesting because I was demonstrating that motor programming worked whereas he could only theorise. At that stage I had no idea of the meaning of motor programming. What followed was a wonderful opportunity for expanding my knowledge.

Alan invited me to work with him and his colleagues in Cambridge. He was just about to go abroad on sabbatical and suggested that I started on a project of some sort. I think it was tactfully meant to discover whether I knew enough to work with them. We were both interested in the subject of innate directionality, so I thought I might try that. The difficulty was in finding subjects, either those who had suffered traumatic brain injuries or had had to change from their preferred writing hand for some other reason. The easiest place to begin was the local stroke club. That proved fascinating in quite a different way, and very useful when I had stroke myself some ten years later. However, what I saw there was worrying, and made me think. The volunteers, pleasant enough ladies, were encouraging the recovering patients to write, often in capital letters, with their unaffected hand. One man was introduced to me as their most successful patient. He confided in me that of course he could now write perfectly well with his stroke-affected hand, but did not want to upset the kind ladies by letting them know.

About the same time, another patient made me think more deeply and helped

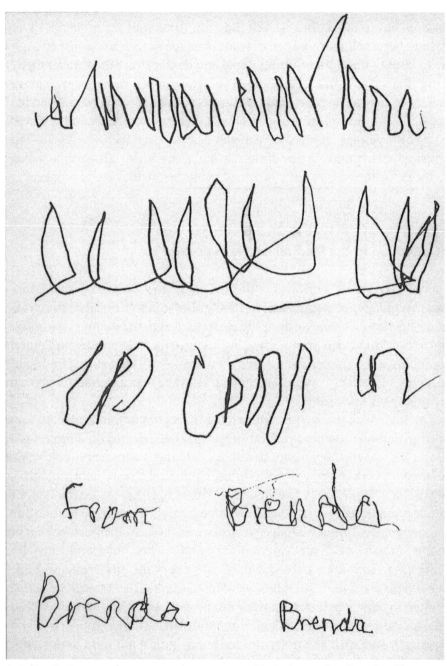

A stroke patient's progress from pattern to letter to name writing in three sessions. Reproduced from *Understanding Stroke*.

me to formulate the idea of mark-making or signature writing as help towards rehabilitation. A teacher, who had suffered a stroke, was in a small nursing home and despaired of ever writing or working again. All she had to help her hand to recover function were two jam jars. She had to transfer buttons from one to the other – not much motivation there. I set her up with a slanting board and got her to make a mark, then a pattern and slowly to make an attempt at her signature. Thus motivated, she must have practised all week, because the next time I saw her the nurses reported with some surprise that she now could use a knife and fork. By the third visit her signature was much improved and apparently she could do much more to help herself. This was the first of many patients who have been motivated to start with marks, then progress to letters and finally a signature, and in doing so have vastly improved their hand function along with their morale.

Back to Cambridge – the joint paper on directionality never got written, but several others followed on various aspects that interested us both. I remember how I had to enter my data (with great difficulty) into their computer. In those days it was enormous and took up a whole room. I was equipped with a very simple BBC Acorn, which was the only computer compatible with their giant. As I have already explained, I had no scientific training, and certainly no idea of statistical analysis. My frequent visits to Cambridge were a real eye-opener. There were often lunchtime meetings where various research topics were discussed. It constantly surprised me that people were interested in any comments that I made – rather hesitantly at first. That was my first experience of the benefit of coming at problems from two very different angles. I was asked, for instance, to advise about a project looking at the value of coloured lenses to help dyslexic pupils. I found that they were testing kids the traditional way, on the speed of their reading using continuous text and whole sentences. I pointed out that this task combined both legibility and comprehension and suggested instead that a series of common words would produce a much more accurate measure. That was adopted, and used thereafter.

A couple of papers on our joint projects were published, the first being an analysis of pen holds that was presented at the second conference of the International Graphonomics Society in Hong Kong. Another memorable one for me was at the CNRS, the National Centre for Scientific Research in Paris. Our work was again on pen hold, and was supposed to be presented by Alan. He had written his talk and had it translated, all ready for him to read. My part was to show slides of the various pen holds that we had analysed. Alan was suddenly taken ill and the whole thing landed in my lap. My conversational French was not too bad, but I had no professional

The alternative or the penhold attributed to Callewaert was illustrated by the Belgian neurologist in his book *Graphologie et Physiologie de L'Ecriture* in 1962. Even then it was not new, as illustrated in the portrait of Eugene Delacroix, reproduced on a French banknote.

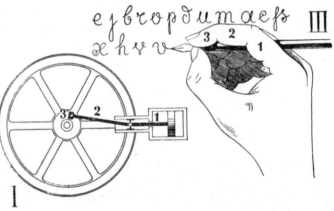

vocabulary at all. I even had to ask a friend, Marie Jean Sedeyn, for the French word for pen hold. She went a bit further and handed me a one hundred franc bank note. On it was illustrated the famous artist Eugene Delacroix, holding his quill in the way that I was talking about – the alternative or Callewaert's pen hold. As she rightly said, this would immediately get the attention of the audience, and somehow I got through the presentation.

This reminds me of how I learned about the neurologist Callewaert. I met an Australian, Murray Everley, who had just completed a handwriting scheme. In it he had mentioned Callewaert's pen hold but did not seem to know what it was, or even who he was. Returning to Europe and recognising the name as Flemish, I applied to my good friend from Belgium, Fernand Baudin who knew everything about the subject. Through him I managed to get a copy of Callewaert's book *Graphologie et Physiologie de L'Ecriture*. I realised at once the logic of his argument and have used this pen hold in countless situations to help patients throughout the years.

Towards a doctoral thesis

In the early 1980s my own research work took another turn. My colleague Briem, was a gifted teacher. He was always trying to push people further on in their work and suggested that I tried to study for a Ph.D. This seemed to me quite impossible. I had never been to university, having left school at fifteen. I was to find out, however, that it was in fact, quite possible. Taking into account my several books and joint published papers, at least two universities were willing to give me a chance. Reading was the obvious choice with their Department of Typography and Graphic Communication. Luckily the publisher, Arnold Wheaton, wanted to use some of my photographs and resulting drawings in a book, so they financed the project – I must have been one of the few people to get anything out of Robert Maxwell. The thesis had the title: *The Joins in Children's Handwriting, and the Effects of Different Models and Teaching Methods.* The idea was partly to provide information to the National Curriculum Council on the state of teaching in our schools. I looked at six primary schools with different models – two with an italic model, two with Marion Richardson and two with no standard model. Then I looked at 100 boys and girls at different stages in local secondary schools.

It was a study in variability, unlike the usual thesis that would prognosticate that what happens in one area would be replicated all over the country. Some of what I found was quite startling, and quite likely was happening all over the country. For instance, as well as the examples of the primary school children's handwriting, I had tested each teacher on how they represented their school model. In addition I took examples of their personal handwriting style. In the case of all the teachers in all six primary schools, except for one individual, they were not teaching the school model at all but versions of their personal script. They had particular problems with italic. Several had bizarre letterforms or serious movement faults that in turn, were being copied by their pupils. The only teacher who could replicate the model was in one of the Marion Richardson schools. She had attended the same school some twenty years previously and had been taught so well then that she still could reproduce the model perfectly.

Another finding was even more interesting. Of the 100 secondary school students, about ten percent were left-handed. It had been suggested that I included a task to investigate the development of signatures. Luckily I had photographed each pupil in action or I might not have been believed. The pupils were asked to write their name at the beginning of the task. It was usually in a childish form of print, seemingly unchanged since an early age. They were then asked to sign their name when they had finished. To my amazement three of the left handed pupils in the 15+ group changed their hand position entirely, from the twisted over the top position, the way that they wrote in the simple style that they used to write their name, to the more conventional way when they signed it. I asked them to alternate these two actions and it was amazing. They did not seem to notice the way they altered their hand position all the time. When I pointed this out to them they all replied in nearly the same words. It was because they could not write fast enough with the over the top grip, and tended to find it painful. This is reported in *The Art and Science of Handwriting*, though I note with dismay that the captions are somewhat misleading.

In those days American research papers were saying that the twisted over the top grip was a neurological indication or result of left-handedness, and should never be interfered with. I had never agreed with that conclusion, and considered it much more likely to be caused by not teaching young children to place their paper to their left side so they could see what they were writing. I know my findings would be termed as only anecdotal but I consider those findings as important. I was already beginning to doubt some research and wonder what methodology could have been used that resulted in their findings, I would have liked to have carried out further work in this fascinating area but there was just not enough time.

There was plenty more too. I was still pretty naive when it came to academic matters, and had had very little supervision or advice during the four years while writing my thesis. When it came to a viva I had no idea what to expect and I nearly came unstuck. I had better not describe what happened for fear of being sued! Gaining the title of Doctor was a bit unreal, but I genuinely felt that the subject deserved recognition. I was 57 by then, and if nothing else this illustrates that it is seldom too late to do what you think is important.

The Curriculum Council were sent a copy of the thesis but they must have either ignored or lost it. However, two or three years later I met the relevant person in the ladies room at a conference. She commissioned a report, and then, in 1992, I presented to the council. It had to be written in the format that they requested and anyhow they did not pay a lot of notice to my recommendations. The only one of my suggestions I that I noticed in later publications was that children should be equipped with two levels of writing before leaving primary school – a slower one for other people to read, and a faster less perfect one so that they were ready for note taking. As they never offered to pay me for all the work, I reproduced the whole report in *The Art and Science of Handwriting* in 1993. If you should discern a slight scepticism in my attitude to the whole system, you would not be mistaken.

Things were developing at such a speed in the 1980s that it is difficult to remember in which order they occurred. Looking at my CV, the first work on Sassoon Primary typeface, my appointment to a post in the Department of Psychology at Great Ormond St Hospital, and another job at the National Hospital for Nervous Diseases, as it was then called, were all dated 1983.

Typeface design

I was back at the teacher's centre one day, dealing with some handwriting problem, when the same teacher who had given me advice about local primary schools before, addressed me in these unforgettable words, 'Rosemary, you know all sorts of odd things, can you tell me why my problem readers can read one page of their reading book and not the next?'. It was quite easy to show her how the first six pages of the book were not justified, some words were equally spaced along the line, but for some reason the following ones were not. With a large print size and short lines the spacing was then so erratic that many short words became so close together that they appeared as one. It is no wonder that some readers, who already had enough problems with reading, were having difficulty.

This made me wonder what was recommended as the optimum word spacing for children. I was surprised to find that no research had been done with actual children, though several experts had expressed their own views. I felt that, as I was in and out of schools all the time, it would not be too difficult to try and find out something about this. Then the real question arose – what typeface or faces would be the most suitable to use for these early readers? Again, to my amazement, I could find no research that had been done in this field. That does not mean that people did not have their own views on the subject. One such expert told me that everyone knew that Times Roman was the best for the purpose. I could not have disagreed more as many of the letters in that typeface, though ideal for adults, are unsuitable and not easily recognisable for young children. Furthermore, I was told that I would not be able to get any reliable data from children. It was a challenge that I could not resist.

I was not, and had never intended to be a type designer, although I had been involved in letterforms for so many years. I had been interested in display faces as a packaging designer but had paid little attention to text fonts, but this was something different. I would be the first to admit that neither my data nor my methods were at a scientific level. They did, however, find out what was wanted and eventually supplied the clues that led to a typeface suited to children's needs. I had already decided that testing children in a formal situation did not work too well. Insecure children were even more tense and performed even more poorly than usual. I also wanted whoever did the testing to have no preconceived ideas that might influence the pupils. I made some preliminary enquiries, and one of the most puzzling comments that I heard came from some teachers of dyslexic children. They told me that their children said that they liked Times Italic. That seemed a bit odd, as I would not have thought it would be particularly legible.

I made out some testing sheets using four different levels of spacing and four different typefaces. The typefaces chosen were Times Roman, Times Italic and two sans serifs, one upright and one slanting. These I handed out to several teachers in different schools in different parts of the country. I could not specify exactly how they were used, as the work had to fit in with their curriculum. Done really thoroughly it would have been pretty time-consuming as each level of spacing would need to be tested with each typeface.

The results trickled in over period of time. For spacing the results were just common sense. Those with reading problems liked wide word-spacing, some needed as much as new sentence new line. Wide spacing annoyed good readers. It would therefore be up to publishers to pay attention to the standard of their prospective readers. The typeface results were much more interesting. Overall, Times Roman was the least favoured and Times Italic came fairly near the top. I cannot remember after so many years whether it was the teachers, or whether I asked some children why they favoured Times Italic, but their answer was very useful. They said that what they called the flick-up at the base of the letter bonded the letters of a word together.

That was the most important and original element to be incorporated into my typeface. I thought about what else contributed to making the shape of a word clearer to young readers. Over the years the ascending and descending strokes of typefaces had been reduced in order to fit more lines onto a page. The first thing that I decided to do was to slightly increase those strokes to accentuate the word shape. The next thing was more complex. I had to make the typeface more child friendly – not only in the obvious ways of altering the letters 'a' and 'g'. Some children had described to teachers how they found some typefaces cruel or unfriendly. It seemed that they were aware of the atmosphere of type, unlike adults who were no longer aware of such things having perhaps been saturated by too much exposure. It is not easy to put into words how this was done. I made the letters rounder and let them express the movement of letters, to make them more familiar and child-friendly, and of course added those 'flick-ups' or what I termed 'exit strokes'.

It is a designer's job to do such things but this was one more thing that seemed incomprehensible to those in other fields of interest. I remember mentioning this in a presentation to psychologists at a conference in Brussels. To show how little many others understood about such things a prominent psychologist stood up and said 'Rosemary, don't tell me that you can express an emotion through letterforms'. I suppose that I answered with something fairly tactful then, but later on I have written in several places, including *The Power of Letterforms* in 2015, this comment: 'For those involved in letterforms their field is as creative as sculpture is to the sculptor. The form and line of a letter is as sensitive as the line quality in a drawing and as individual as the interpretation of colour and light are to a painter.'

I drew up my design, but then what next? I had no way to digitize it or test it out. I took my design to Monotype who had helped me to produce the test sheets. There I learned something else new. My contact there told me not to bring a new design there without first copyrighting it. That sounded complicated but all it meant was that I should put my signature under the design, write the word copyrighted and the date. At that time they did not have the capacity (or desire) to take it on, so back to square one.

I was going to a conference in Germany where I knew there would be many colleagues. I intended to offer it to my university department if they wanted it, but I was surprised at the reception I got. One person said, 'whatever makes you think that you can do anything that we cannot? You are not even a type designer'. Another colleague told me not to pay any attention and said it was a good idea. He said he knew people who could digitize it – but the price he mentioned was way beyond what I could afford – and even then how could I market it? We went on some sort of outing later on, to an exhibition, I think. In the bus, still smarting from the reception I had received, I told the pleasant young man sitting beside me all about it. He immediately offered to do the job at half of a very reasonable price, in exchange for half the profits. I said that I did not know if there would be any profit – but quickly accepted the offer.

That was my extremely fortunate introduction to Adrian Williams, a young type designer who then had a son at primary school, and even more luckily lived fairly near to me. We have now worked together for over 30 years in a happy partnership, the project could never have materialized without his part in drawing up, digitizing and marketing our fonts – as they developed. The original font, Sassoon Primary, was finished in 1985 when something else very opportune occurred. A colleague, Mike

A selection of the fonts designed for educational purposes.

Daines, had been approached by the firm, Research Machines, who in those days supplied most of the schools throughout the country with their computers. They needed help with obtaining an educational typeface. As it was not his area of interest he very kindly sent them to me. I seem to remember that we gave RM exclusive use of the font for a year, and it certainly paid off. We were rewarded with a lucrative contract that lasted some 25 more years. This gave the original font enormous exposure and publicity. In all the years we have never had to do any advertising.

The education department of Apple were also very interested in using it on those of their computers aimed at schools, but unfortunately the way that their machines were manufactured meant that it was impossible to separate computers for adults from those intended for children. However, they gave me a large, impressive printer that lasted me for most of twenty years.

The next development was a clamour from publishers and then teachers, to alter the font to be suitable to represent handwriting. At first I was very reluctant, being averse to having my name involved in any handwriting model. However the letters were non-stylistic, and suggested the movement of letters that is so important. Additionally, there were obvious advantages for letters for reading and letters for writing to be alike. We made a few alterations and a family of fonts suitable for teaching handwriting was designed. Looking back I realise how formative this was in my constant battle against the use of print script. The static models that had been prescribed for so many years inhibited the development of flowing joined up handwriting. In the intervening years those handwriting fonts have outsold the reading ones. I can remember a visiting professor from India coming to visit me, and showing me what he thought was the English national model. I had to tell him that it certainly was not so, just my own typeface.

Several years later I met a colleague, James Hartley, who was a professor of the psychology of type, at a conference. He approached me fairly diffidently and told me that he hoped I would not be offended but his students, who were doing comparative studies using my original typeface, felt a bit patronised by Sassoon Primary. Far from being upset, I was thrilled. This meant that the juvenile vibes designed into the font works really stood out. At his suggestion another family of fonts was developed, using the same legibility factors, but for adults. Adrian is now using the same design principles and applying them to letterforms for other writing systems, starting with Cyrillic and Greek.

The typefaces led to another fortunate introduction. I was invited to a conference by a group called Writing and Computers. It was held in Brighton, not far from my home.

I did not want to give a presentation but agreed to do a poster display. I nipped down one morning and set this up, just in time for the participants to come out from their lunch. I think they were mostly American, and they stopped in front of my display. There was an immediate chorus of, 'I never thought typefaces were important'. This comment caught the attention of a man who had been sitting quietly in the corner. He was Masoud Yazdani, who had recently set up his own academic publishing company, Intellect. 'If they know so little about the subject I think we had better have a book about it' said he. I did not know enough about the subject then, but with contributions from several colleagues, *Computers and Typography* came into being, followed some years later by *Computers and Typography 2*. Masoud became a good friend, and was the most ethical of publishers. He promised to keep books in print as long as possible, and never put up the price. Sadly he died very young, but with his encouragement I had written, and he had published, eight of my more serious books between 1993 and 2011.

Enough about typefaces, except to say that, it was not for me to do any comparative studies between mine and other typefaces. I only know of one, though there may be more by now, and that was an absolute disaster, even more so because it was meant to decide what was the best type for the partially sighted. The person doing it seemingly had no knowledge of the subject. Having slightly lengthened the ascending and descending strokes to accentuate the word shape, the point size of my typeface had been altered. She either ignored this or just did not know that fact. On her test sheet all the typefaces were produced in 18 point. Therefore mine was at least one third smaller in body size and the sentence that was produced was at least a third shorter than all the others. The results were hardly unexpected!

Part 3

The wider implications of handwriting problems

The medical aspects of handwriting

When my first book on calligraphy was published I received a very polite and beautifully written letter asking me for a sample of my italic handwriting – on the supposition that all scribes wrote italic. I wrote an equally polite but less beautiful reply in my usual relaxed handwriting saying that although I could write a professional italic hand my personal script was far from it. Then I forgot all about it. Quite a few years later I went to an informal talk on handwriting by a friend, Christopher Jarman. I must have exchanged names with the man who was sitting next to me because he identified himself as the writer of that letter. He asked me to have a drink afterwards, saying he wanted to talk to me about something. What he wanted to say was that he was head of the Department of Psychology at London's Great Ormond Street Hospital, and that he had been following my work, and would like me to come and work with him. So began the start of my more serious involvement in the more medical aspects of handwriting

This appointment was a huge step forward in my work, and I have always considered it a real privilege to be offered this position and to gain such valuable experience. Richard Lansdowne was an amazing person to work with. I learned a great deal from the occasions when I saw him in action. I remember him telling children that it was their body so they could probably tell him what was wrong. This was so different from the usual formal testing and prognosticating methods of

The Hospitals for Sick Children *Special Health Authority*

GREAT ORMOND STREET, LONDON WC1N 3JH
Telephone: 01-405 9200
Telegrams: GREAT LONDON WC1

PATRON: HER MAJESTY THE QUEEN

CHAIRMAN: MRS. C. BOND. S.R.N., S St. J.
HOUSE GOVERNOR: R. G. B. MILCHEM. F.C.I.S. M.B.I.M

LM/JFG   21 February 1984

Mrs R Sassoon
34 Witches Lane
Sevenoaks
KENT

Dear Mrs Sassoon

I am pleased to confirm your honorary appointment with The Hospitals for Sick
Children as a handwriting consultant.

This appointment will last from November 1983.
During this period you will be seeing children and advising their teachers on
work.
You will be responsible   Dr R Lansdown, Chief Psychologist.

Terms & Conditions

During your placement with this Authority you will be expected to abide by
the policies and procedures of the Group, copies of which may be obtained
from your Head of Department or can be seen in the Personnel Department.

Health & Safety

Your attention is drawn to your responsibility for taking reasonable care for
the Health and safety of yourself and of other persons who may be affected by
your acts or omissions at work and by your co-operation in assisting in carrying
out duties with regard to Health and Safety at work. You shall not intentionally
or recklessly interfere with, or misuse, anything provided in the interests of
health, safety or welfare. In this respect your attention is drawn to the
Departmental Code of Practice which is designed to secure safety in work practices
and in the handling of materials and equipment, a copy of which, your Head of
Department will be happy to show you.

Confidentiality

In the course of your appointment with this Authority, you may come into possession
of information concerning the private affairs of the general public. Such
information must always be treated as confidential. Similarly, information
concerning the affairs of this Authority must not be communicated to the press or
any such other unauthorised person or persons.

Con .... / ...

A letter from The Hospitals for Sick Children, Great Ormond Street. It confirmed my appointment
as a handwriting consultant.

other professionals. He suggested interesting subjects or hobbies for those in trouble, thereby sometimes transforming children's lives. However, I could not do what he had originally wanted me to do. That was to train his staff in my so-called methods. To have a circle of people around taking notes as I tried to help a scared kid, really would not work. It would only result in more tension and make matters worse. I had long discovered that there was no magical method involved. Each patient presented a different problem and required an individual approach and solution.

I preferred to see only one, or perhaps two patients a session. It was intense and draining to sink oneself into a child's problems and try to relax them, to find a way into their confidence so that they would confide in me about their real worries. Only then could I get to the root of their trouble and suggest a solution to their handwriting and other difficulties. Constant uninformed criticism as well as being stigmatised by an incorrect diagnosis could so affect a pupil's confidence, that it could stifle and destroy creativity and affect the child's whole academic progress. Incidentally I would always try to first have the patient seen by the excellent orthoptist in the hospital, being already aware of how many children were affected by unnoticed visual problems.

I am not able to cite details of any hospital patients. All that I can say is that they were diverse, ranging from the relatively simple to solve to the extremely complex. I was often sent to colleagues in other hospitals with a particularly problematic patient, via the useful network of specialists and post-graduates. This practice even extended to others overseas. I was travelling extensively by then and this led to some interesting meetings in such places as Hong Kong and Singapore. Such was the influence of a hospital such as Great Ormond Street. It should be explained that oddly enough, I was never offered any payment for this work. All my hospital posts, then and subsequently, were entirely honorary. There seemed to be no funding for such work. I was never paid, even for travel expenses, and never charged a patient who came to me in any other way. I continued at the hospital for several years, going in about once a fortnight. Sadly this wonderful opportunity eventually came to an end when Richard Lansdowne was promoted to another post, I think with the World Health Organisation. This did not stop patients being referred to me by hospitals and this even turned out to be beneficial.

When children came to my home it was easier to get them relaxed. Some kind of distraction technique was usually required, and it is amazing what even a packet of chocolate biscuits can do. Later I acquired, from a patient who had grown out of it, a most wonderful relaxer in the form of a battery driven toy dragon. It was meant to be a present for my grandchildren, but served a much more useful purpose, It could be

This battery driven dragon was the ideal thing to distract and relax tense and worried children.

made to walk, growl and even pretend to bite the hand of anyone playing with it. When distracted by that toy dragon children confided incredible tales of maltreatment and misjudgements that they had experienced. They told of incidents that their parents knew nothing about. It was sometimes hard to listen to their stories and try to alleviate their suffering.

I hope this person will forgive me for telling his story so many years later, but I feel that it is important that people should understand how some children had been treated. He suffered from a form of Tourettes and I was puzzled by the referral that stated that he was unable to write at all because it included a very good drawing surrounded by a pattern resembling letters that seemed to rather contradict the diagnosis. Relaxed and fortified by the usual chocolate biscuits, he related his shocking story. When he 'touretted' his teacher put sticking plaster over his mouth and tied his hands behind his back. He was so traumatised by this he had not been able to learn to write (and what else I did not find out) with her in charge. His mother was horrified as this was the first she had heard of this. I found it difficult to know what to say. I asked if that teacher was still in the school, thinking that if so she should be prosecuted, but she had left the job. Sometimes humour works best, and all I could think of to say was that it was a nuisance that she was no longer there or he could have sued her and made a lot of money. This was not the kind of comment that would have been possible in a hospital situation but it appealed to him, and he laughed. We retired to my kitchen table where, after a while, relaxed and relieved, he managed to write quite adequately. He had a slight relapse in secondary school but when I last heard of him, several years ago, he was finishing university. He was one of the very few patients whose family kept contact with me.

Apart from the hospitals, schools sent me their problem pupils. It often needed no specialist training or testing to solve these cases, just common sense. Although of course I accept that there are real and serious cases of dyslexia, dyspraxia, autism and other conditions, I have become, over the years, more and more sceptical about the methods of testing, diagnosing and stigmatizing of so many children. Some problems were so simple that anyone with a bit of imagination could have fixed them. A young boy in a school for the physically handicapped had strangely webbed fingers. He was longing to be able to colour his pictures. He had a hole punctured between two of his fingers, but all he was given was a simple black lead to enable him to make his mark. The local stationery shop provided a set of ultra thin coloured biro refills. They did the job perfectly adequately and made him happy. You can understand why I never refused to see anyone. I had this desperate urge to communicate in writing or any way that I could, issues that I considered major injustices. To my way of thinking it often only needed people to start being observant, treating children as intelligent beings, listening to what they were saying and then trying to understand what it means to be unable to write and so often to be blamed for it. This has can have a lasting effect on their education and their feeling of self-worth.

It was not only one or two hospitals that continued to refer patients – I have no idea how many of the others heard of me. Cases also came from therapists. Let me explain: I ran courses for paediatric therapists, both physio and occupational, from a centre (I cannot remember its name) situated just at the end of Great Ormond Street. Subsequently, if any of the participants came across anything really puzzling they tended to contact me for advice. There were unusual cases such as a very bright boy with arthrogryposis. He had taught himself to use a computer using only his little fingers, but longed to write. Together we solved it by interlacing the fingers of both hands so he could manage a pen. His delight was well worth the trip half way across the country to see him at his local hospital.

The same therapist presented me with an even more interesting case, something I could never have learned from a book. A teenager was experiencing sudden behavioural problems and the observant therapist had an idea that the boy was writing with the wrong hand. She was not sure, so she asked if I could come and see him. The boy was relieved when I told him that what she suspected seemed likely. Then he relaxed enough to relate his strange experience. He said he thought that he was going mad. When he wrote with his right hand (the one he had been taught to use at school) there was always a considerable delay between his thinking and his getting his thoughts down on paper. When he tried to write with his left hand this hesitation did not occur. When confirmed, therefore, that he should use his left hand his whole attitude altered. However I had to warn him that he might write more slowly for a while as his hand became more accustomed to the different action. I have never met another similar case nor read any relevant research, so cannot provide any explanation.

More often than not I went to see such patients wherever they were. Our three daughters had by then left home, and my husband had taken early retirement from his university post to research and write about his special interest – Sumer, and other very early civilisations. He never minded driving me halfway across the country. There was always a library somewhere where he could shelter and read. As always, no one else seemed to be dealing with these serious cases of handwriting problems and what implications they might have for the child's future. It was obviously not deemed worthy of any funding. It seemed to me only ethical to gain as much knowledge as possible, if not how could I justify lecturing and writing about the subject? Anyhow each of these serious problems taught me more – what it was like for that boy made to write with the wrong hand to find real difficulties in his teenage years, or what were the consequences of a serious neurological condition that altered basic innate directionality? The satisfaction of this work was fantastic.

Around the same time this medical aspect of handwriting had expanded. Whether in one of the several books I had written by then, or whether in a presentation, I had mentioned the problem of extreme pain that I had found in teenagers' hands. This occurred when they had to write more extensively or faster, often under tension, and could become serious enough to make it impossible to write at all. It was not only in England that I had observed this, but also in my old school in New York and in high achieving students in Hong Kong and in Australia. Whatever the cause, I had coined the phrase Juvenile Writer's Cramp. The correct name of this condition is focal dystonia. It is caused by overuse and misuse of muscles. This had previously been considered exclusively an adult problem. Somehow neurologists had picked this up and started to ask me to see their adult patients.

I well remember the first patient that I was asked to see was at a London hospital. It was an unusual case but it was not too difficult to sort out what was needed. What happened next was more difficult to deal with. The specialist who had asked me for help came in. Instead of being pleased that his patient's problems had been solved he was angry. He said that that was not what he had wanted at all. He wanted a set of rules that he could apply to all his patients, to which I replied that that was impossible. Each patient appeared with different problems and needed careful diagnosis and treatment. This did not stop him from sending me further patients later on.

I think it was when I was giving a presentation to the Eastern Motor Group in Cambridge that someone from the hospital that in those days was called the Hospital for Nervous Diseases, now called the Hospital for Neurology and Neurosurgery, attended. As a result I was offered a post there (again honorary) to see patients at specialists' request. Initially I was supposed to see writer's cramp patients who previously had only been treated with botulinum toxin. This had to be given frequently and only dealt with the obvious symptoms without dealing with the real problem. Although focal dystonia appears to be a neurological condition, it is not so. Testing in the hospital before I saw any patient could prove that it was an acquired condition that could be helped in other ways, as I had already found out with teenagers.

This is not a quick-fix situation with adults, as I was reminded recently when I found some old videos of me treating patients. It would have gone far beyond just finding them an alternative and more comfortable pen hold, paper position and posture that might alleviate the problem with the teenagers. First, usually using some distraction technique, I would have to persuade them to produce a letter, or at least some mark with their distorted, tense hands. Then it was usually a tricky matter of trying to explain that basically there was nothing wrong with them, and the way back was literally in their own hands. They had been certain that they had some incurable neurological condition that was beginning to impinge on their whole lives.

Slowly they might unwind and such marks as they could produce would improve. It was heartening when at last someone realised that they could write after all – but I had to say it might be a while before they could relax enough to write happily once more. I don't really like using the phrase, but writer's cramp had become a serious psychological problem, probably over some time. It had resulted in some people losing their jobs and more than one appointment was often needed. One impediment to the acceptance of what I was doing was that I could not supply scientific evidence to support my methods. That is true. As I have written elsewhere, I valued the solving of a patient's problems more highly than providing evidence to validate my techniques (even if that were possible).

Plenty more patients with different conditions such as multiple sclerosis and other debilitating conditions were loaded on to me. It was heartening to devise some means of enabling those patients to carry on using their hands, if only for a little longer. Sometimes the occupational therapists did not agree with my methods but that did not worry me as long as it benefitted the patient, after all they themselves had done nothing effective. It is a pity that, for the sake of confidentiality, I cannot describe the treatment of any hospital patients in detail.

One day a rather arrogant young neurologist, who had never even bothered to come and see what I was doing, announced that he intended to recall my patients every few months to see if my methods had had a lasting effect. I tried to explain that if the patients were called back into a hospital situation it would probably make things worse by reconfirming the medical aspects of their worries. Instead I suggested that I should deliver a presentation of my work so that everyone might understand what I was doing. This was a success but had disastrous results. Professor Marsden, the head of the hospital was very interested, and called me into his office to hear more. He asked me what my position was and I explained. He was horrified and said that I would not be covered by their insurance if anything went wrong and many of their patients were litigious (and some more that I wont repeat). So I asked if he could arrange for me to be covered by their insurance but he said he could not as I was not a neurologist. He asked a psychologist if she could help but she was even more adamant. She asked why should she be asked do something as I certainly was not a psychologist. So ended a fascinating few years where I had once again hugely enlarged my experience.

I had been trying for some time to get everyone to understand the importance of getting patients to make their mark. I had hoped that signature writing might be added to the list of daily living skills, but to no avail. It is a basic human need. In addition, working towards a signature provides the best motivation to practise, and in doing so improves hand function along the way. To the doctor or therapist it would also provide a visible record of improvement in the patient.

Writing and travelling

I would not like this publication to appear like an advertisement for any books that I have written. But somehow those books are a major part of my own story. At first I found it necessary to fill a gap in knowledge, but it was so large that many of my subsequent books were requests from publishers. I remember a pleasant phone call in about 1989 from someone asking to come and see me about handwriting. In my innocence I thought it was a teacher or someone similar. Instead it was Roger Crowley from the publisher Stanley Thornes, wanting two more books. *Handwriting The Way to Teach it* is still in print 26 years later, although now with another publisher. The

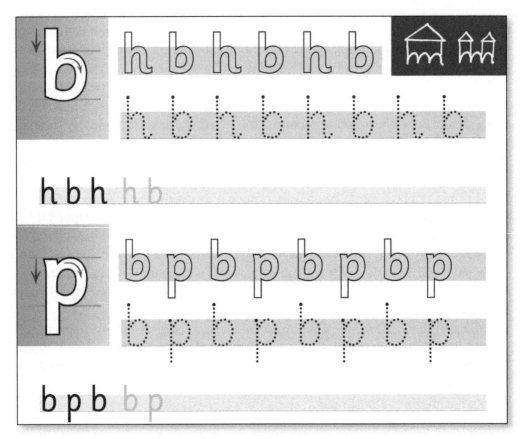

Early exercises from *Write For You*, a series of copybooks designed to teach Arabic students who are learning English as a foreign language.

other book, *Handwriting A New Perspective*, a more serious one and, in my opinion, the better of the two, never sold well and was soon out of print.

Some of the many publications do indeed chart the progress of my work. In other cases, books that were commissioned dragged me into quite new areas that required considerable research and took me into new fields. One example of that was a commission to write five copybooks of 60 pages each and a teacher's manual. This project was to teach Arabic-speaking students to learn to write our alphabet. The letterform part did not present a great difficulty. It was the actual content – what to include and what to leave out to make the series meaningful, that took more time and effort. The books ended up combining vocabulary, commonly used phrases, useful grammar etc, down to such thing as how to write a letter and address an envelope.

I look at the many books that I have produced over the last 30 years, and I cannot but wonder how they all came about. Sometimes I read one of the early and find it hard to believe that I wrote it. Esther Aresty was right in that it becomes almost an addiction. What began with a simple book on calligraphy became a part of my life. As I have said, it was more because publishers kept coming and commissioning books, not because I was writing books and then searching for a publisher. Yet it was more than that. I had rediscovered, at the age of fifty, the real pleasure of writing that had been squashed out of me at the age of thirteen. With my children leaving home, came that well known surge of renewed energy. It became a habit to wake up early in the morning and think of what needed to be written during the day, then get up and get it out of my system. That still goes on, and is the way that I work in my 80s. Of course writing is creative in the same way as designing – in fact very similar. I am a very visual person and for me a book becomes almost a solid entity to be fashioned into shape.

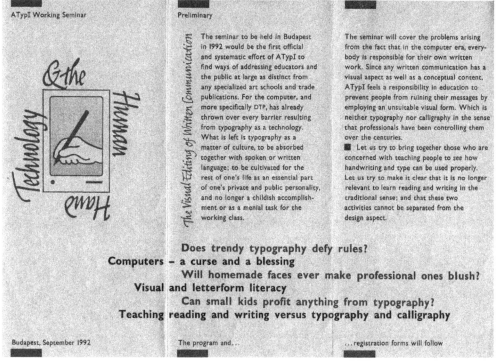

Details of an interesting seminar by ATypI conference held in Budapest in 1992.

I have called this section 'Writing and travelling' because those two aspects got involved sometimes. I had so many fascinating trips during the next 30 years. Most of them were to international conferences, necessitating the writing of a paper that eventually would be published. To an established academic these constant conferences, both abroad and at home, would have been quite normal. To me they were again a revelation, an incredible opportunity to meet colleagues and expand my areas of interest. Luckily the British Council often financed these trips because I was not part of any particular university. So I got, for instance, to Hungary, Norway, Sweden and all over Europe, the USA, Canada and best of all, China and Argentina.

I have found my 1985 report to The British Council concerning my visit to Hong Kong and Beijing. In those days there were very few Europeans in the country, and I was the only British person in the group. We travelled right across the country visiting universities on the way. The constant request was for more contact with British universities, more books and research material. It was obvious from my report that they were not at that time getting the hoped for help from the British Council. Most of all they wanted access to British universities for the best of their post-graduate students. They could go to Russia to study and were given grants to the USA, but they wanted to go to England. Now that was where I could be of help, because my husband ran the external department of London University. We were both invited back the following year and by that time he had arranged for several of their best students to find places, and we ended up with several lasting friendships.

Not everything was so serious. A visit was arranged for me to visit the artist Fan Tsue Tsuan who lived in one of the traditional courtyard houses in Beijing. He had two requests. One was to see if I could introduce him to someone in England who would co-author a book on his favourite subject, the art of the peony. I did my best through the various London art schools but do not know what the outcome was. The other request I could not help with. It was to find a gallery to put on an exhibition of his paintings. Anyhow he presented me with two of his beautiful paintings. One of which sits on my wall as I write this book lending an atmosphere of tranquillity and beauty. Luckily we have a young cousin studying Chinese who, with difficulty, read the accompanying characters. Not surprisingly the inscription is a poem on the beauty of peonies.

There is one minor incident worth remembering. Somewhere along the way we visited a primary school. Something caught my notice. A girl was practising her characters on standard sheets that were marked out in somewhere between ten and twenty squares. A single character was repeated in each one. I noticed her work because in the first few squares the character was written perfectly, likewise in the last few, but in between they were not anywhere near as good. To me it was obvious that she could write the character perfectly well but became bored or tired after a while then recovering, relieved that the exercise was nearly complete. I pointed out the difference in line quality only to be met with comments such as 'how can you possibly tell when you do not even know the language?'. I remarked on the difference in the line quality that would be evident whatever the script. That certainly interested my companion. He was Henry Kao, otherwise known as Gao Shen Ren. A good friend, he was a professor at Hong Kong University and his particular interest was the psychology of Chinese calligraphy. I very much doubt however, that my remarks made any difference at all in how the school taught their pupils.

We travelled to Australia each year where two of our daughters then lived. We usually stopped on the way in Malaysia, Singapore or Thailand, for a brief holiday. Then, as the introduction network took over, some of these destinations became interesting places to work. I cannot help mentioning one place that was pure pleasure and not much work. One day, about twenty years ago, while waiting for

Painting of a peony by Fan Tsue Tsuan given to me during my visit to Beijing.

my husband to pick me up at Sevenoaks station, I noticed that, on a basement level, there was the office of the Solomon Island tourist agent. Going inside it looked so interesting that it became our next stopover. A tiny island off Guadalcanal called Tivanipupu housed a small resort. The whole island was magical and unspoilt – the fish seemed to swim towards us in the sea rather than away. Years later, Prince William and Kate visited it on their honeymoon but I expect it had changed a bit by then. The only other visitor at that time was an interesting islander, who arranged an outing by canoe to a tiny school on an even smaller island.

Back to work – in Singapore I was asked by a physiotherapist to see one of her aphasic stroke patients who seemed not to be responding to treatment. I will never forget that case. At the small nursing home he was laying on his bed, silent, inert and looking miserable. I asked the nurse if they gave him, an intelligent man, any way of choosing his food or anything. Her brusque reply was that they could not afford such luxuries, so I explained I that I only meant a piece of paper with simple illustrations. That was the first time that the patient's eyes lit up, so I asked if anyone had ever tried to see if he could write. Her reply was shocking as she expressed her view (rather forcibly) that he was not capable of anything. I demanded a pencil and a piece of paper, the patient immediately became active, sat up and wrote a whole line of Chinese characters with his undamaged left hand – not an easy task. Sadly none of us could read it!

As always for me, this case led directly to some work I did with a young designer, Guillermina Noel. She was allotted to look after me, as was usual practice, on my arrival in Buenos Aires where I was to present a paper at a conference there. Her father had had a stroke and was left aphasic and additionally was unable to communicate through writing. Together we designed a series of personal cards illustrating his possible needs, to give him a wide choice. I added a series of emoticons (as I called them) so he could let people know how he was feeling. Many speech therapists work this way, with large volumes of illustrations, but what we were trying to do was to show how families could help. Another conference followed in Canada, in 2003, appropriately called 'Designing Effective Communications'. That was where together we presented this work. My part was called 'Interactive Iconic Communication to Help Those Suffering from Aphasia'. I asked how we could help when the capability to communicate by speech, which we take for granted is lost, when words make no sense and even letters are unrecognisable. I described that when personal communication disintegrates it is more a matter of bridging a communication abyss than creating a communication space.

Guillermina named our system the 'aphasiboard'. She designed seven sheets of illustrations as a personal iconography. She reported on the effect on her father and family. We were not suggesting that everyone could produce such professional illustrations but between any two people any mark or basic picture can be given a meaning. This presentation had an incredibly emotional effect on the audience. I think that most of them had never heard of aphasia and its consequences for patients. Quite honesty neither had I until I suffered a stroke myself a few years before this conference.

In Hong Kong it was again schools. In an American school I saw the worst possible teaching of handwriting to young children with no consideration of the correct movement of letters, whereas in the Chinese schools it was more a matter of the intense pressure of the educational system taking a toll on the students hands. In Malaysia, a wonderful woman called Asiah Abu Samah, who I think was director of education, asked me to survey and report on some of their schools. There were Chinese, Malay and Indian schools each with their different writing systems. I do not know what good I did but I learned a lot. This contributed to my growing interest in how students who wrote in their own writing system learned to adapt to writing in another, very different one. This seemed to be another area that had seldom, if ever been seriously considered.

I already had collected quite a lot of examples, and questioned children and adults alike about their difficulties either with specific letters or some other aspect. I remember that my examples of Burmese writing, along with useful suggestions came from a student on an aeroplane, plus a compatriot whom I met in a London bookshop. There was plenty of research to do, and more abstract things to consider. This led, in 1995 to my book *The Acquisition of a Second Writing System*. In it I wrote 'Manuals and copybooks seem to assume that a suitable method to instruct a non- Latin writer, of any age, would be the same as that used to teach any English speaking infant just entering school'.

In some cases that might be appropriate, but this way of thinking ignores both the special skills that experienced writers of some nationalities may have, as well as the special problems that might arise in other cases. It also ignores the retraining of the hand and sometimes the whole body that is needed where a new direction of writing is involved'. Another thing that worried me was that a student's ability might be underestimated through their immature script in another writing system. This could even happen in the same writing system when tackling a different language where translation and spelling might cause tension and hesitation that in turn could cause their script to deteriorate. I think that this book somehow led to the commissioning of those copybooks for Arabic students.

Somehow I wrote too much to fit into one book. My tiresome, restless and inquisitive mind had led me astray into looking at iconographies as well as second writing systems, as possible cross-cultural means of communication, and there was enough left over for half of another book. My friend Albertine Gaur helped out with the history part of *Signs, Symbols and Icons*, in 1997, while I concentrated and had fun with everything from all kinds of icons in general use today, and the possibilities opening up for computer-generated icons, to symbol systems for special needs and the visually impaired or deaf signers and much more.

Then along came quite a different request. A group of people, whose interest was in cataloguing cemeteries, came across the place where Marion Richardson was buried. She had lived and taught for many years in Dudley Girls High School where she had formulated her revolutionary method of teaching art and later handwriting. The Dudley Museum was planning a memorial exhibition about her work, and they contacted me to write her biography. I had long been an admirer of her work, not so much what she did in Dudley, as her later work in London where she wrote her famous work, *Handwriting and Handwriting Patterns*. It was quite a different kind of writing task, researching someone's life and I was lucky enough even to be able to trace some of her former students. I would have enjoyed doing more in this line of work – but there is just not enough time in one life! Unfortunately the curator of the museum left and the exhibition never took place, so I do not imagine the book *Marion Richardson, Her Life and Contribution to Handwriting* sold as well as expected.

As well as books there were incessant articles to write on a wide variety of subjects. I have a bundle of publications that I have kept. They include in *The Graphologist*, 'The relationship between pen, penhold and the individual'; 'A letterers journey' in *Forum, Journal of the Letter Exchange*; 'Through the eyes of a child, perception and type design' in *The Australian Journal of Remedial Education*; and in a typographic journal there was an article 'A designer but not a type designer'. This finished with the prophetic sentence 'If I ever get round to writing my autobiography I intend to call it *By Accident or Design*, just what I am doing now. One of my favourite articles was written for *Growthpoint, Journal of Social and Therapeutic Horticulture*. It was called 'A stroke survivor's kitchen garden'.

From what you have read so far you might well think that I spent all my time when at home, on the computer. That leaves out the whole of the other side of my life. This was probably a matter of both nature and nurture, because I have always been a very keen gardener as were my father with his shrubs and bulbs, and my mother with her fruit and vegetables. We chose the house that we lived in for 50 years partly because of the large greenhouse that led off the back veranda. Anyone else would probably have converted it into a luxury sun lounge. For me it provided food nearly all the year

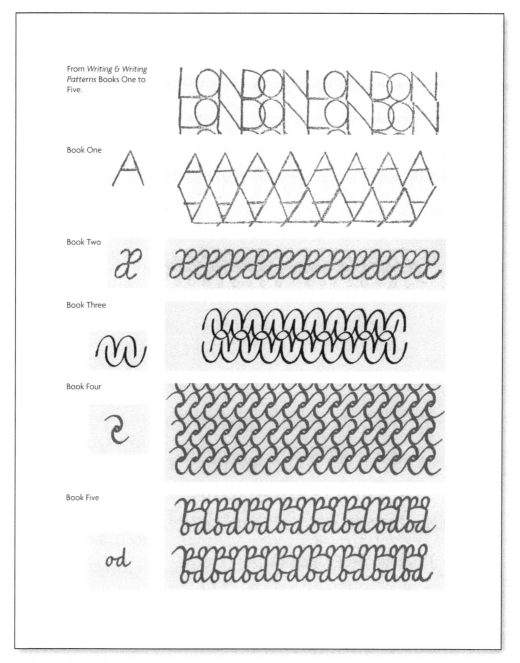

From *Writing & Writing Patterns* Books One to Five.

Book One

Book Two

Book Three

Book Four

Book Five

A selection of typical letter patterns from Marion Richardson's *Writing & Writing Patterns*, Books One to Five.
From *Marion Richardson: Her life and Contribution to Handwriting*.

round, with salads, tomatoes, peppers, and cucumbers etc, and it was also a home to all the seedlings that populated the garden as spring arrived. Fruit of all sorts abounded, and more attention could be paid to everything as the children grew up. Visitors used to comment rather sourly, 'it is all right for you, you have green fingers' as if that were a nasty inherited disease. We seemed to have passed on that gene to the next generation too.

How did that all fit in to my working life? When at home I would set to work in the morning and write until I had achieved what I wanted to do for the day, and having exhausted that side of myself, I would then go to the greenhouse or up the garden to work and relax. It was the perfect combination and eventually turned into yet another, but very different type of book, *Fruit, Grow, Cook and Preserve* because, of course, cooking your own produce is the other part of the fun. And then at the age of 67 I had a stroke.

Part 4

A stroke, getting older and some conclusions

The effects of a stroke

Admittedly I was rushing round the world and working pretty hard for someone in their late 60s, but my stroke was entirely unnecessary. I had always had rather high blood pressure and at last I was given medication. The first drug made me strangely ill. My doctor said I was asking for a heart attack, working so hard, and sent me to a specialist. That man looked at me as if I were a child and told me all that was wrong was that the drug had given me asthma! A second drug was just as bad in another way, and when I went to report that, the GP announced that I was not all that bad and he could not be bothered with me any more. Those were his exact, unforgettable words. Several weeks later I had a stroke.

I do not intend to make this too personal an account, but this was the second time in my life that working too hard had been blamed for something quite different. The first time, over forty years earlier, I was carted off to hospital the very next day with a form of meningitis, after a visit to a GP who had made similar comments when I reported some strange symptoms. These two cases taught me that you cannot always trust doctors. Certainly 60 years ago, and even twenty, there were still people who seemed to suspect women with an active professional life, and liked to blame any ills on their busy working life. The one who caused my stroke struck me off his list and erased my records from the practice computer in case I sued him.

Anyhow, having a stroke was not the disaster that it can be for many people.

It taught me a lot. I was very lucky in that I had worked quite a bit in the field, so was spared the shock that many people experience. I was lying in bed, paralysed down one side when a young man in a white coat, equipped with a clipboard and pen sat down beside me. He asked me 'on a count of one to ten how depressed are you?' 'Not at all, I find it all quite interesting', I replied. He probably thought I was deranged, and anyhow beat a hasty retreat. But it was true. The hands of most of the patients that I had dealt with had recovered their function fairly quickly, so that was what I hoped for, not knowing that legs were much more problematic. I still think it a bad idea to suggest to patients that they should be depressed – frightened, shocked, worried, yes, but clinically depressed is quite another matter.

There was another thing that interested me much more that day. I had listened to several talks on neural plasticity in the past and I wanted to test to see if I could make it work for me. The only movement I had on my right side was just in the tips of my fingers and I tried to see what the power of thought could do. I cannot remember how long it took, but sometime that day I was able to move all my fingers and my hand and my wrist as well. The physiotherapists were very interested, but what I termed my 'message' went no further and I was not able to get through to communicate with my elbow for nearly two years to make it straighten.

The hospital was in the last stages of disrepair, as it awaited the building of a new regional one. The ward was a dumping ground for any elderly patient unwanted elsewhere. The staff managed as best they could in difficult circumstances. The physiotherapists were excellent, young Bobath trained girls. The occupational therapists were just the opposite, seemingly only capable of showing patients how to make tea. I wanted to know if I would be able to use a computer with one hand, and spied one in corner. 'Oh we do not know anything about such things' was the reply. Ever since then I have attempted, where ever and when ever possible, for the disabled patients to have some training on the computers that would be such a help to them in their future lives. Of course, the next generation will not need that, being already fully competent.

As for speech therapists, there were none at all in the hospital. That is how I learned of the plight of aphasic patients. Nurses talked over them to each other as they made their bed, occasionally doctors talked about them, but no one talked to them. On the other side of the ward a patient could be heard saying occasionally in a sort of stuttering whisper 'what has happened to me'. Several years later a taxi driver told me of his experience as an aphasic patient in hospital. Again people talked over him and about him but never to him. One day he heard a doctor say 'call for an ambulance, we cannot do anything more for him'. He was sure that he was going home to die, though of course he was being transferred for rehabilitation. Years later, and obviously fully recovered, he could still remember his distress.

Later on when I gave lectures to nurses and others, often through the Stroke Association, this lack of communication was the first thing I stressed. One day a specialist in one particular area, exclaimed in some distress, that that was just what they did in her hospital – stood around a bed and discussed a patient's needs without thinking of ever addressing the unfortunate occupant. 'I will never do it again' she said. That statement made much more of an impression than anything I could say. Just because someone cannot speak, even temporarily, does not necessarily mean they cannot hear and understand – although sometimes it can but that does not excuse not attempting to communicate.

After communication, the next important issue is, as I see it, motivation. It is not so easy to know how to impart this. Maybe it is explaining that everything you try to do for yourself (within the bounds of safety) aids recovery. In the end, whether you have much treatment or not, it is up to you alone whether you get better or not. That seems a harsh thing to say, because not everyone has the willpower, or strength of mind to face the long struggle to get going again. My own method of self-motivation, for what it is worth, worked like this: in those early days at home, every morning, to give me a reason for getting up, I set myself some small task for the day that I should be able to do. I suppose it was something of a challenge, but gave me some satisfaction. I have always believed, and still do, that if I do not constantly push myself forward, I would go backwards.

Throughout my stay in hospital, and so many times in different situations, I heard the destructive word 'plateau' used. It was meant to describe the optimum time that any improvement could be expected in a stroke patient's rehabilitation. Apart from being totally inaccurate – you can go on improving for as long as you believe in yourself and keep on trying – it could be very demoralizing and counterproductive. I remember a ten-year-old boy reporting that he had been told not to expect any improvement after two years, but luckily he had ignored what his doctor had said. Personal experience has taught me that certain things can be helped to function better even after nearly twenty years when dealt with by informed neuro-physiotherapists. I would have the use of the word 'plateau' banned.

My physiotherapists warned me that I would not have much help once I left the regional hospital, and urged me to stay longer. I did not believe them, but they were right. Without a GP, as I had been struck off the practice list, I had little help. At home

I managed to get out of a wheelchair, and onto a stick fairly soon, determined not to be beaten by the stroke. It was then that writing came to my rescue. I would have been much more fed up with being disabled, had it not been that I could still go on writing. It was not too difficult to go ahead, initially one-handed, and finish *Handwriting of the Twentieth Century*, which turned out to be one of my best books. And so it continued, usually a book a year, but I was soon on my feet, aided by my stick, and travelling again. It was easier to go anywhere in the world by air, with the help to be had at airports with wheelchairs, than it was to go to London by train.

There was another fortunate occurrence. One day when visiting the regional hospital, for quite another purpose, I was approached by my old friend the physiotherapist. She asked if I could spare them a day. What was happening was that the team from Salisbury Hospital were giving them a training day on the use of their newly developed Functional Electronic Stimulus (FES) and they needed to demonstrate it on someone. As a result I was invited to Salisbury to be fitted with one of their appliances, to deal with what they called my dropped foot. This was the first time I had even heard of that term – a very common result of stroke. It was a success in more ways than one. As Alan Wing has written in *Understanding Stroke*, there are huge benefits for stroke patients – in terms of morale building, if nothing else – being involved in research.

I suppose I did contribute a little because I was very stubborn and believed that I myself should take a part in retraining my muscles. I did not want to be continuously dependent on a device to help me, so asked if I could use the FES off and on. The reply was that they did not know if there was a carry over effect. That I understood to mean that there might be no further strengthening of my muscles when the stimulator was switched off. Evidently this was not so, as the combined effort of my own exercise and the machine worked well. I heard that in some cases that was what was recommended in the future.

I found out by experience what effect motivation (or desperation) plus adrenaline could have. One instance was when I got off the plane in Buenos Aires accompanied by a Swiss colleague, for that conference. Two young colleagues greeted us. They told us to go and get changed and to prepare for a morning of sightseeing. I protested, to no avail, saying that I could not walk far at all. Determined though, I managed somehow with my stick, and had a fantastic day in the markets and fun area of the city. There were couples dancing the tango all over the place and what looked like statues but came alive as you passed them, stalls of all sorts, wonderful bookshops and much more. I wish I could remember the name of the district.

I had read a couple of the current books on strokes. There were one or two personal accounts that might prove inspiring, but not much use in a general sense, and I presume that there were also medical books. There was nothing that bridged the gap for patients, carers and health professionals looking at the situation from various perspectives. After two years it seemed the right time to produce a much-needed book combining my own observations and experiences with contributions from colleagues from various different specialist areas to supplement them. So the first edition of *Understanding Stroke* came into being. Writing this sort of book means taking on certain responsibilities. Requests for help and advice that poured in were, I suppose, the obvious result. It increased my own knowledge, particularly of the long-term effects of stroke, and the patchy help available to people in some parts of the country.

One case sticks in my memory. Someone telephoned, having heard about me from a charity. I never even knew her name but her story was disturbing. Her fist had become so crippled and tight that her nails were digging in to the palm of her hand. All her doctor said was to congratulate her for being so brave in such circumstances. Not much help there! She lived in the west of England and all that I could suggest was that she should consult the nearest neurologist or alternatively Salisbury District Hospital to see if an FES (Functional Electronic Stimulus) would help. I heard later that a neurologist had prescribed botulinum toxin and that it had successfully, if maybe only just temporarily, dealt with her problem. More talks to give and more articles to write led to a second edition of *Understanding Stroke* ten years later. I kept the part that I had written of the initial effects of stroke but extended it to discuss long-term effects – not necessarily personal. The contributors both therapists, researchers as well as others, mostly updated their chapters.

I never completely neglected the other side of my life – lettering. Long ago I had observed in some others (not all) the disadvantages of continuing scribal work, especially for reproduction, say into your 70s, when hands tend to be a bit shakier. As far as teaching, I had already become much more interested in helping people to develop their own personal letterforms, rather than traditional calligraphy. Luckily, as it happened, this did not entail any demonstrating on my part, as, somewhat ironically, I had never fully recovered the full use of my right hand. I was still able to carry out courses around the world, enjoying myself and doing what I loved, promoting lettering and travelling. All this is chronicled in *Lettering from Formal to Informal*, in such a way that anyone can copy my teaching technique. It includes examples from a course I ran Australia and another one in Rome's Pallazzo delle Esposizioni.

As I have said I am a great believer in the concept of 'use it or lose it', and find it incredibly fortunate to be able to go on working into my 80s. Many of my colleagues in letterforms find that they also can teach, write and carry on with work long after most people would have retired. Things are made easier by modern technology. In the past I gave a presentation to a conference in Mexico via Skype, when they had used up all their finance elsewhere and had nothing left for airfares. Just recently I was invited to address a conference in Spain. Now living in Australia (which they had not realised) made it difficult. They wanted a video and one of my grandchildren obliged and produced it for me! The Internet disguises both distance and age, making almost anything possible. We need no longer to be victims of ageism (though it might be a shock when an elderly visage greets them on screen).

Conclusions

It has been an interesting task, delving into my life and career, learning a bit more about myself as it proceeded. I am still left to wonder how and why this sequence of events came about, and what can be learned from it. Luck and pure coincidences must have played a part – but there must be more. Having an unusual training, as a classical scribe, was definitely relevant. Even knowing the history of writing and different techniques helped sometimes. While enjoying mastering the skill, I did not have the disciplined temperament needed for it as a career. That strict traditional training, however, influenced my whole life's work, from lettering through handwriting problems, both educational and medical, to type design.

Having an unusual skill but being able to use it more widely in quite different areas, is a useful way into a career. Combining this with the problem-solving attitude developed as a designer makes a good combination. Perhaps that is the first suggestion. If you have an unusual skill, or set of skills, look for some different field where they can add a new perspective or dimension to your own work or that of others. In a progressively more technological world this could be even more valuable. What part was played by my own nature or character? Maybe that should be left to others to decide. Perhaps the fact that I had had so little formal training left me, perforce, with a more open and enquiring and maybe hungry mind. My doctoral thesis satisfied part of that and demonstrated that if I could do it, then anyone can do anything they want today, whatever their age.

I was lucky to have had the opportunity of experiencing that wonderful and satisfying feeling that comes with solving someone's problem or alleviating their pain. It made me wonder whether, in other circumstances, a career as a doctor would have been a good idea. However I have to admit that I would probably never have had the patience for such a lengthy training. Yes, impatience is another feature of my character. I also do not like waste. This perhaps was the consequence of years of rationing when young, and seeing real hunger in Africa later on. Many things that I have seen could be classified as waste – waste of human potential through misdiagnosis or neglect of a pupil's problems, for instance. Reading through this text I can also see how the media, in the form of newspapers and radio etc, played the part in helping me to find first a job when desperate and afterwards led to other opportunities. Today the Internet would be even more effective.

There is no denying that I enjoyed the life of a designer and it suited me at an early age. It is also a useful career when you have children as you can do so much of your work at home. I have a very visual imagination and the aspect of continuous problem solving really suited me. Left alone that is what I probably would have remained. It was a pleasant if rather self indulgent and satisfying life – although unlikely to make a fortune. However, I do not think that you stop thinking as a designer or can suppress that way of problem solving whatever other path you may follow. The questioning attitude that becomes part of your personality remains invaluable, whatever you do – although it sometimes gets you into trouble. Anyhow, once a designer always a designer! In the end perhaps the most lasting of my projects was the design of a family of typefaces meant originally to make reading easier for young children. Inadvertently, as I have mentioned earlier, this also had a significant effect on the teaching of handwriting. Publishers such as Cambridge University Press adopted Sassoon Primary for major handwriting schemes, influencing others to add exit stroke to their letterforms, thus hastening the end of print script.

I might have had doubts, even feelings of insecurity about my lack of education, especially when my daughters began university, but who knows? I am pretty sure that one day I would have rediscovered the joy of writing, but I could hardly have imagined that I would write as much, anyhow what would I have written about without so many different experiences? I cannot see myself writing fiction. When reluctantly I accepted the challenge of looking at what was happening about handwriting problems in schools, it did not necessarily mean the end of designing. What I found was so serious, however, that it seemed worth altering the emphasis of my work. This was the first of several examples of a task that so obviously needed tackling that no one else deemed worthy of their attention. I sometimes wonder what made me take on the challenges that arose. Part of it seemed to me the injustice on the part of those who might have helped to solve the plight of those who needed help, but ignored it. Maybe I was beginning to consider that lettering was not enough to fill a life. The decision was certainly made easier by the timing. My children were leaving home resulting in that surge of energy that happens at that time, leaving more time available for work and travel.

With handwriting, not much has changed in the intervening 35 years and in some ways the problems are even more serious. With the teaching being phased out in several countries, and a basic form of communication in danger of being lost, still no one is looking at the task in a universally thorough way. I am now sometimes asked to write articles on the subject of 'Is Handwriting Dead?' It will be if we do not understand how to teach it in a meaningful way, adaptable to changing conditions, making it an easier, less painful more palatable and therefore relevant to the next generation of computer orientated students. Before I left for Australia I was asked to prepare a short course for student teachers. Whether this was ever taken up I do not know. Anyhow, this is not the place to give a detailed lecture. It is high time to hand this problem over to the next generation. I can only hope that they will consider the individual and their hands and body plus the basic movement of letters, more than an arbitrarily imposed model or standard pen-hold, without considering the consequences. Earlier on, when talking about rehabilitation I talked about wanting the term 'plateau' eliminated. I would not mind the term 'neat' going the same way – or at least being replaced in most cases by the more essential and less destructive word 'legible'.

When I started to look into the more medical aspects of handwriting problems, again I found that few people had considered this subject worthy of much thought – nor have they done so up until the present day. With children, I have already reported that the first thing I had noticed in schools was pain. The pain started from early on and progressed through the years so that eventually, through tension and the need for speed, it developed into a form of writer's cramp. I found the same problems all round the world and still do. I remember an expensive boys school in Australia where, when asked if they found handwriting to be painful, almost all the teenage boys put up their hands. Their master replied that of course handwriting hurt – it was a discipline. Not much hope of understanding or help for that class.

Then I found ridiculous issues such as children being labelled dyslexic or dysgraphic when their only problems were that they needed a pair of glasses, or criticised because they could not replicate their school's model. That is only the first stage. No one seemed to understand how being unable to write adequately, often through no fault of their own, or even just poor teaching, affected the whole child. Their written trace reflected back their failure, usually augmented by constant criticism. It affected their self-esteem (you cannot hide poor writing), their academic progress and ultimately their happiness. It became a psychological issue, but dealt with in a sensitive and understanding way it could be alleviated quite easily. I soon found how unsatisfactory were the standard tests in this area. The specialist teachers, psychologists and others should not depend on and hide behind their professional training that has never dealt adequately with such matters. Those who are so sure that they are right, without further thought, do inestimable harm. It often needs only close observation, questioning and lots of common sense, to help young children and even older students – but adults needed more.

It is a basic human need to make your mark. When you are disabled being unable to sign your name is a real deprivation, even in this age of computers. I had experienced this previously with stroke patients and a few others, but it was only when faced with multiple cases in a hospital situation that I realised how serious the problem could be. Dystonia patients needed a distraction technique to demonstrate that they were able to write, then assurance that the remedy was literally in their own hands. Those suffering from degenerative conditions needed different help. They needed practical, but often unconventional, techniques to help sustain their mark-making facilities a little longer. Sometimes however, it only needed a little luck. Recently, in Australia, where I now live, I was faced with a relatively young woman seriously affected by multiple sclerosis who had long since given up hope of even signing her name on her Christmas cards. All she needed was the confidence to try a slanted board propped on her lap, a different pen hold and she was off. Her screams of delight worried the other therapists where we were, until they found out the cause. What I found then, and still do today, is that therapists either do not know, or do not care about these aspects of disability. All the emphasis is on mobility, not that it is unimportant. Daily living skills, such as making a cup of tea are stressed but never signature writing. There is no understanding of its benefits towards the motivation to rehabilitate, or even its use as a diagnostic aid. The human trace is an invaluable clue to the condition and therefore the progress or otherwise of a patient. There is little that I can do about it other than to pass on my ideas to whoever will listen. I have no formal qualifications, as is sometimes pointed out to me. As I have said before, for me, the pleasure that many patients display when their problem is solved or at least alleviated makes this work so worthwhile. I can still remember what M C Oliver used to say to us in his lettering classes over 60 years ago: 'if you ever have a student who is better than you, think yourself lucky'. I had just one, but then I did not teach for long. I know what he meant, do not resent them and hold them back. That applies to whatever field you work in. I would like to think someone would pick up my work with disabled hands, and take it forward, but I will now probably never know.

The effect of contact with serious researchers, and what I learned by working with the Medical Research Council, awakened something in me. In addition to problem solving I felt a real thirst for knowledge, and I needed to conduct more serious research of my own. To find that I could apply for a doctorate, in spite of leaving school at the age of fifteen, was a complete surprise. The four years working on that study led me to other research in the field that sometimes had findings that did not seem right to me. I had better not quote any names here, but what I will say is that looking at their methodology it was not surprising that I found their results unlikely. I have become pretty cynical in my old age!

The only major project that I embarked on with no outside pressure or influence was into suitably legible typefaces for children. It was just a feeling that something so important needed to be investigated. That whole project taught me, as if I needed to know by then, how little the specific needs of children were considered. I have tried to explain, in articles and presentations, that type designers have both opportunities and responsibilities. There are opportunities, even lucrative ones, out there for typefaces designed for special purposes and directed at special needs. The responsibilities involve careful research into those users special requirements, and not going the tempting route of just designing what you think is the right solution, and justifying it afterwards.

So what other lessons can be learned from all this? One thing that surprised me, already reported, but needs repeating, became apparent at the lunchtime meetings at the MRC where people discussed their work. After a while I hesitantly offered a few comments, and to my surprise these were sometimes considered useful. This continued to happen as increasingly I began working with pretty high-level doctors. These were people that I respected and I felt fortunate to be working with them. As they got to know me, and what I did, quite often they would say things like 'why can you see things about my patients that I myself have not observed' Again it appeared that coming from a completely different background, with a different set of skills (and I might add, an open mind) might be an advantage at any level, when solving problems.

Now I want to consider more serious and perhaps controversial thoughts. There are certain issues that, as I have no affiliations I feel free to voice. As time went on I could not help noticing how restrictive some in the medical or allied professions (teachers as well) found their training. They relied on tests and preconceived ideas limiting their ability to use their common sense to diagnose and solve problems. Arrogance seemed to become a defensive mechanism, to the detriment of their patients and pupils, especially those with the kind of problems that I have had to deal with. I may have had plenty of experience but no formal training at all. So much of what I found effective was often just a matter of observation and common sense, taking patients own comments and situation seriously. I have been reminded that the public are increasingly litigious, prone to sue at the slightest hint of a mistake. Therefore perhaps this limits anything that might be considered experimental or not scientifically proven. In addition, feeling that I might be too judgemental, I have discussed this matter with many people in different fields. I was surprised that so many people agreed with this prevalence of arrogance. I can only hope the next generation will be more open-minded.

The problem that I always come back to is why all the issues that were loaded on to me were not thought important enough for any one else to consider. My work involved no magical scientific discovery, only issues and techniques that made a lot of lives easier. I recall a rather dismissive letter from a specialist who wanted scientific proof that my so-called method worked. It said 'whenever we find something that looks like a good new treatment we have to find ways of testing it. Some of us are lucky, in that we have the training and facilities to test out our own treatments.' I could not supply what several people expressively asked for: a set progression of treatment or a pathway, that fashionable term, to be followed in the case of every patient. Quite the opposite, each patient presented with different problems and needed individual treatment. I could never supply scientific evidence of success without recalling countless patients to assess the ongoing improvement in their condition. In my consideration, even if that were possible, a medical recall would have set them back all too often, by bringing back their fears and tensions.

All I can hope is that there is enough information left for others to carry on this work in the future. My handwriting examples, photographs etc., are safely stored in archives in case people might find them useful in the future when there is not much material left to study. My collection of books, copybooks and papers, many of which had been handed on to me by others as they grew older and no longer could keep them, are in various other university libraries and archives. It was very satisfying to find places for all this material. Personally I have had a fascinating life, and cannot really think of anything in my career that I would have altered. Now in my mid-eighties, carrying on working as much as I can in different fields, I still see a few patients and try to solve their problems. Their therapists, as usual, ask what training I have had. I then have to tell them my field was in letterforms and I have had no medical training – and then I still have to explain how and why an odd journey led me from my origins as a designer into so many different fields.

References

Aresty, E: 1964 *The Delectable Past*. Simon and Schuster.

Callewaert, H: 1962 *Graphologie et Physiologie de L'Écriture*. Nauwelaerts, Louvain.

Mahoney, D: 1981 *The Craft of Calligraphy*. The Pelham Press.

Richardson, M: 1935. *Writing and Writing Patterns*. University of London Press.

Sassoon, R: 1983 *The Practical Guide to Calligraphy*. Thames and Hudson.

Sassoon, R: 1986. *Helping Your Handwriting*. Arnold Wheaton.

Sassoon, R: 1986. *Teach Yourself Handwriting*. Hodder and Stoughton
     (later title altered to *Improve Your Handwriting* and *Helping Your Handwriting*).

Sassoon, R: 1988 *The Joins in Children's Handwriting, and the Effects of Different Models and Teaching Methods*. University of Reading.

Sassoon, R: 1990 *Handwriting; A New Perspective*. Stanley Thornes.

Sassoon, R: 1990. *Handwriting; The Way to Teach it*. Stanley Thornes.
     Republished by Paul Chapman – Sage.

Sassoon, R: 1993 *Computers and Typography*. Intellect.

Sassoon, R: 1993. *The Art and Science of Handwriting*. Intellect.

Sassoon R: 1995 *The Acquisition of a Second Writing System*. Intellect.

Sassoon, R and Gaur, A: 1997 *Signs, Symbols and Icons*. Intellect.

Sassoon, R: 1999. *Handwriting of the Twentieth Century*. Routledge Republished in 2007 by Intellect.

Sassoon, R: 2002. *Understanding Stroke*. Pardoe Blacker Publishing.

Sassoon, R: 2009. *Lettering From Formal to Informal*. A&C Black then 2015 The Unicorn Press.

Sassoon, R: 2006 *Handwriting Problems in the Secondary School*. Paul Chapman – Sage.

Sassoon, R: 2008. *Write For Life*. McGraw Hill. Five copybooks plus teacher's book.

Sassoon, R: 2011. *Marion Richardson, Her Life and Contribution to Handwriting*. Intellect.

Sassoon, R: 2013. *Understanding Stroke*. Revised edition The Book Guild.

Sassoon, R: 2015 *The Power of Letterforms*. The Unicorn Press.

Sassoon, R: 2016. *Fruit, grow cook and preserve your own*. The Book Guild.

Sassoon, R: 2016. *Designing Textiles in the Mid 20th Century*. The Book Guild.

Schwalbe, W: 2012 *The End of Your Life Book Club*. Hodder and Stoughton.